SAFAR-E-SHAHADAT THE JOURNEY OF SHAHADAT

A Day-to-Day Narrative Depicting the Unmatched
Love and Bravery of December 1704

NARRATED BY BHAI HARPAL SINGH HEAD GRANTHI
GURUDWARA SRI FATEHGARH SAHIB
Translated by Tejkaran Kaur

Safar-E-Shahadat: The Journey of Shahadat

ISBN: 978-1-963353-90-7 (Print)

ISBN: 978-1-963353-91-4 (E-book)

Printed in the USA by Sikh Reference Library USA

"Safar-e-Shahadat da, bara safar anokha see. Jaalum vi dadda see, te darad bhi choakha see"- Bhai Harpal Singh

The journey of Shahadat was a very unique journey. The cruelty was unprecedented and the depth of pain unmatched."

This book is dedicated to the family of creation, to all people from all faiths and walks of life. It is dedicated to all the brave souls who have sacrificed their life to uplift humanity, and to all those who continue to fight for human rights and justice. My deepest heartfelt gratitude is to Guru Gobind Singh Ji, Mata Gujri Ji, Baba Ajit Singh Ji, Baba Jujhar Singh Ji, Baba Zorawar Singh Ji, Baba Fateh Singh Ji, and the entire Khalsa Panth, without the grace of whom this would not be possible. I also want to thank my mother, Sardarni Harbans Kaur Ji, and my father, Sardar Nirmal Singh Ji, for guiding me to the Guru's path.

TABLE OF CONTENTS

Foreward..x

INTRODUCTION: EMBARKING ON THE JOURNEY- A note from the translator..1

HISTORICAL BACKGROUND: THE JOURNEY FROM TALWANDI TO ANANDPUR SAHIB...............................16

 A Lover is a Fighter..17

 Not a Single Moghul Soldier Turned Blind.....................20

 Defining "Shahadat": When love shatters the limits of our body...23

 The First Accounts of Shahadat in Sikh History.................28

 Tyrants should sit at the foot of your bed..........................32

 Giving your life to protect what you don't believe in...........35

 The Army of Compassion and the City of Bliss.................37

 A thorn in the eye of cruelty...41

 Leaving Anandpur Sahib out of Respect for Hinduism and Islam...44

PART ONE: THE NIGHT OF 7 POH AT GURUDWARA CHHANN BABA KUMA MASKHI JI..48

 Prayer is more precious than life...................................49

 A promise broken..51

 The love of Baba Kuma Maskhi Ji..................................53

A promise kept by a virtuous daughter………...……………………56

A love unmatched…………………...…………………….....60

PART TWO: THE NIGHT OF 8 POH AT GURUDWARA ATTACK
SAHIB……………………………………………………...64

Kehri Becomes Saheri………………………………………65

The Battle of Chamkaur Sahib Begins…………………….....68

The request of Baba Ajit Singh Ji………...………………….74

You will steer the boat of the Panth………...………………..78

I belong to the Khalsa……………………………...……...80

Do you have cloth for all my children?.......................................82

The bed of thorns of my beloved is the best……………...…….83

A brave young girl becomes the final shaheed of Chamkaur
Sahib……………………………………………………...85

PART THREE: THE NIGHT OF 9 POH GURUDWARA KOTWALI
SAHIB…………………………………………………...…86

Police Brutality towards Mother Gujri Ji and the Sahibzaday…...87

Finding Freedom Behind Bars……………………………...87

The cowardly masands turn their back on the Guru…………….92

PART FOUR: THE NIGHT OF 10th POH AT THANDA BURJ,
GURUDWARA FATEHGARH SAHIB……………………….94

Who are these small children under the Peepal tree?....................95

Guru Gobind Singh Ji's Muslim Children……………………96

The first night in the Cold Tower……………………...……...98

The kindness of Baba Moti Ram Mehra Ji............................100

Mother Gujri Ji prepares her beloved grandchildren for court...103

First Day in Court (11 Poh)...105

Second Day in Court (12 Poh)..108

And they will remove every trace of cruelty from this Earth.....114

The Cries of Princess Zaina Begum....................................118

The most expensive land in the world.................................119

Sirhind becomes a pile of bricks.......................................119

EPILOGUE: THEIR JOURNEY IS NOW OUR JOURNEY. HAVE
WE KEPT THE FAITH?..124

FOREWORD

In the rich tapestry of history, there are threads that are woven with the fibers of sacrifice, courage, and unwavering commitment to truth. The echoes of those who dared to challenge oppression still resonate through time, guiding us along a path illuminated by the radiant spirit of righteousness. The profound narrative of Poh 1704 in Sikh history stands as a testament to the indomitable will of the Khalsa. This narrative is retold in the sacred words of Baba Zorawar Singh Ji and Baba Fateh Singh Ji, which were eloquently narrated by Hakeem Allah Yaar Khaan Jogi Ji.

The book titled "Shafer-E-Shahadat: The Journey of Shahadat" presents a moving account of the Safar-E-Shahadat movement, which invites us to relive the unforgettable days of December. It narrates how the power of love and sacrifice helped defeat tyranny. The journey of Baba Ajit Singh Ji, Baba Jujhar Singh Ji, Baba Zorawar Singh Ji, and Baba Fateh Singh Ji, alongside Mata Gujri Ji, is a story of courage, revolution, and sacrifice that remains unparalleled in the history of humankind.

This book serves as a guiding light, not only delving into the historical events of Poh 1704 but, more importantly, unraveling the profound why behind what. It transcends the boundaries of time, offering timeless lessons that echo through the corridors of our existence. The principles that motivated the Sikhs then are the very values they fight for today, and this book implores us to grasp the essence of their struggle, to comprehend the purpose behind their sacrifices. In our quest to understand, we embark on a journey—a journey of Shahadat, of bravery, love, and unwavering commitment. This is not merely a recounting of events but an invitation to connect with the spirit of those who laid down their lives for justice and righteousness. The narrative extends beyond the physical, resonating with the universal struggle against evil and cruelty that persists today.

Bhai Harpal Singh Ji's Safar-E-Shahadat movement calls upon Sikhs around the world to follow the path of the Sahibzaday. Translated by Tejkaran Kaur, the book presents Bhai Harpal Singh Ji's katha and serves as a doorway for English-speaking Sikhs to rediscover their cultural origins. The book is an invitation to experience the sense of pride that runs deep within those who are responsible for carrying forward the legacy of Guru Nanak Dev Ji.

As President of Sikh Reference Library USA, it is my earnest hope that this English translation becomes a beacon for Sikhs, inspiring them to reclaim their identity and join the collective journey. The narrative is not confined to the past; it is a living, breathing testament to the eternal struggle for truth and justice. May the readers be moved not only to understand but to actively participate in the ongoing Safar-E-Shahadat—the journey that transcends time, connecting us all in a tapestry of shared sacrifice and unwavering commitment to the divine principles of Sikhi.

Rupinder Kaur
President
Sikh Reference Library USA

INTRODUCTION: EMBARKING ON THE JOURNEY- A NOTE FROM THE TRANSLATOR

INTRODUCTION: EMBARKING ON THE JOURNEY- A note from the translator

"Those who try to erase truth will themselves be erased from this world,

For God does not fear the strength and splendor of kings,

Listen to these words with your ears and heart,

We speak the truth, and truth is the tongue of God."[1][2]

- The words of Baba Zorawar Singh Ji and Baba Fateh Singh Ji in the court of Wazir Khan as narrated by Hakeem Allah Yaar Khaan Jogi Ji[3],

---

[1] "Shaheedan-e-Wafa," by Hakeem Allah Yaar Khan Jogi Ji, stanza 96.

[2] Here I use the word "God" to refer to the being that is nameless, formless, and beyond all description, as discussed in Guru Granth Sahib Ji. The Sikh concept of God is a single divine entity that created everything, an entity free from fear and hate, who loves all of creation limitlessly, and lives within all. God is the same for all of creation, regardless of the fact that people from different religions may refer to God using different names. The word "God," is used here to reference the "1", described in all of Gurbani (the word Gurbani means the word of the Guru, Gurbani is a term used to describe the writings in Guru Granth Sahib Ji).

[3] Hakeem Allah Yaar Khan Jogi (1870-1956) was a Muslim poet who wrote poems in love and praise of the Gurus, the Sahibzaday, and great Gursikhs. Jogi Ji was excommunicated from Islam and shunned for praising the Sahibzaday and Gurus in his poems. On his death bed, Jogi Ji was offered the chance to be welcomed back into the faith and die a Muslim, if he apologized for writing these poems. Jogi Ji was told he would obtain paradise if he died as a Muslim. Hakeem Allah Yaar Khan Jogi Ji refused and said that his paradise was in Guru Gobind Singh Ji's arms, which were open and waiting for him. Centuries later, his devotion filled language helps us envision the feats of Poh 1704.

1

The last days of December, the shortest and darkest days of the year, hold the most glorious feats of history. The darkness of these days reminds us of the darkness which engulfed India in Poh[4] 1704. The bitter cold reminds us of the pain faced by Mother (Mata) Gujri Ji and the Sahibzaday. It reminds us of the cruelty of King Aurangzeb and Wazir Khan. The barrenness of winter is symbolic of the hopelessness of an enslaved nation, ruled by terror. It is during these cold, dark, and hopeless days, that the Khalsa[5], the army of saints, rose up and challenged the darkness in a way that none have ever dared. The darkest days of history thus became the canvas for the greatest triumph of compassion. This is the true story of Poh 1704. This is the story of warrior saints who looked death in the eyes with such bravery that even death was afraid. This is a story of love, revolution, courage, kindness, and sacrifice unmatched in the history of the world.

These warriors-saints were members of the Khalsa, the army of compassion. They left their comfortable lives to end human suffering. They did not fight for selfish motives but fought for righteousness and equality. They fought for the dream of Guru Gobind Singh Ji. The dream of

---

[4] Poh is the tenth month of the Punjabi calendar. It starts in the middle of December and lasts until the middle of January. The Journey of Shahadat takes place from around the 6th of Poh until the 13th of Poh, around December 22-28.

[5] The word "Khalsa" is first defined in Guru Granth Sahib Ji, "Says Kabir, they are known as khalsa, whose way of worship is love (Guru Granth Sahib Ji, 654)." This definition predates the first Amrit Sanchar (Khalsa baptism or initiation ceremony of April 1699) and the establishment of the Khalsa Panth in its present form.

turning this world into "haleemee raj", or the "kingdom of compassion." Every country has an army whose loyalty lies to their nation. That army fights for the interests of their country, regardless of whether those interests are just. The Khalsa army's loyalty is not to any country, race, or religion. The Khalsa is the only army in the world whose sole loyalty is to the human cause. The Khalsa is the only army whose goal is to end the unjust suffering of all people, regardless of which country, race, political ideology, or religion they belong to. The Khalsa is an army that stands up for all of creation and sees all people as the beloved children of the same single creator, regardless of their background. The Khalsa army serves the family of creation without any barriers or distinction.

This is the journey of the Khalsa family, the family of Guru Gobind Singh Ji. It is the journey of the four sahibzaday (the beloved biological sons of Guru Gobind Singh Ji), Mata Gujri Ji (the blessed mother of Guru Gobind Singh Ji), and the beloved devotees of the Guru, who are as dear to Guru Gobind Singh Ji as his own children and family. Guru Gobind Singh Ji's beloved sons embody all the qualities that make up a perfect Khalsa soldier. Even the names of the Sahibzaday have deep symbolism.

The word "ajit" means one who cannot be defeated. In order to become a Khalsa, one has to be the master of their mind. Even when times are tough, they must never accept defeat. Gurbani[6] says

---

[6] The word "Gurbani," refers is to the writings of Guru Granth Sahib Ji.

victory is not an outward state but a state of mind. One is not defeated by losing in a competition, they are only defeated when they accept defeat. The first Sikh prayer, Jap Ji Sahib, states "mann jite jag jeet,[7]" which means that by conquering your mind you conquer the world. Guru Gobind Singh Ji taught us "nischai kar apne jeet karo."[8] The word "nischai," refers to a type of confidence[9] that is only found through deep faith in God. This line means that true victory is found in nischai. As long a Sikh does not succumb to darkness or defeat within their heart, that Sikh is victorious. For a Sikh, victory lies in the struggle itself, not only in the outcome. For a Sikh, each day is a battle, A Sikh is not in competition with others, they are in constant competition with themselves. Good and evil will never reconcile. For that reason, a Sikh will always have to be ready to stand up against evil, there will never be a day where their struggle is finished. A Sikh never gives up the fight and that is why they are undefeatable.

---

[7] Guru Granth Sahib Ji, 6

[8] Dasam Bani, 100

[9] Many confuse confidence with ego. In Sikhi, there is a subtle yet important distinction. Ego comes from thinking that we are great, and others are low. Ego is Godless. Gurbani says that God realization cannot exist where there is ego. In contrast, confidence comes from faith in God. It is the feeling that we are unstoppable because we have the grace of the powerful creator on our side. Imagine a young child who is weak and feeble on their own. Yet, when that same child sits on their father's shoulder's they feel like they are on top of the world. Gurbani says "Raaj leela terai naam baniye," which means "when I remember God, I feel like a king." The word "Nischai" refers to the confidence which comes only from great faith. Likewise, many confuse humility with a feeling of inferiority. Those who are connected to God are humble but not inferior.

4

The word "jujhar" means one who fights relentlessly. Life is a struggle. To struggle is to be alive. A Sikh should always strive to uplift themselves and others. Without struggle, one is as good as dead. There is a famous historic incident when 300 villagers came to Baba Banda Singh Bahadur Ji[10], complaining that the chief of their village was being abusive and mistreating them. The villagers asked Baba Banda Singh Bahadur Ji to help free them from the chief. Baba Banda Singh Bahadur Ji asked how many villagers there were in total. The villagers said that there were about 300 of them. Baba Banda Singh Bahadur Ji asked how many chiefs there were. The villagers stated that there was only one chief. Baba Banda Singh Bahadur Ji then said that all 300 villagers should go stand in front of a canon and have someone shoot it. The villagers were shocked at this seemingly sarcastic response. They asked Baba Banda Singh Bahadur why he would say that. Baba Banda Singh Bahadur Ji told them that if 300 of them can't fight against one man and stand up for their own rights, then they are already as good as dead. They have lost the will to fight, and without that a human becomes dead inside. It is important for each Sikh to understand that we are all warriors. We do not need to wait for a leader or someone to help us. We all have the strength; it lies within us ready to be awakened. A corpse relies on pallbearers to carry it. Those who are alive take the lead. They do not wait

---

[10] The brave Sikh general who led the Khalsa to victory and defeated the Moghul Kingdom after the execution of the Sahibzaday. This book will describe Baba Banda Singh Bahadur Ji is more detail.

for others. They find the power within themselves to struggle for their goals.

The word "zorawar" means strength. Sikhs should be strong. Strength does not come from exerting power over others. Strength comes from forbearance. It comes from exerting power over oneself. Guru Granth Sahib Ji says that a saint should have the forbearance, the great vastness, of trees.[11] A tree bears winds and storms. It gives fruit and shelter to all, even to those who want to cut it. The ocean is vast and open, it takes everything in without distinction. Water flows and is soft, yet it has the strength to cut through mountains. A truly strong person is not a bully. A strong person does not scare others. According to Guru Teg Bahadur Ji[12], a true devotee of God should "neither make anyone afraid nor be afraid of anyone."[13] Strength does not come from a person's brute or stubbornness. It comes from endurance. It comes falling at the feet of God. Only those who fall at the feet of God are able to proudly stand tall in all of life's challenges.

The word "fateh" means victory. Guru Gobind Singh Ji knew that those who have victory in their hearts and on their lips are the ones who have victory in the battlefield. Sun Tzu is famous for saying that every battle is won before it is ever fought, if one believes in their victory.[14] The Sikh

---

[11] Guru Granth Sahib Ji, 1381
[12] Father of Guru Gobind Singh Ji, Ninth Guru of the Sikhs- This book will go into more detail about Guru Teg Bahadur Ji and his sacrifice.
[13] Guru Granth Sahib Ji, 1427
[14] The Art of War, 3

greeting is a reminder of victory. When two Sikhs meet, they say "Waheguru Ji ka Khalsa, Waheguru Ji ki Fateh." This means that the pure hearted ones, the Khalsa, belong to God and victory is also God's. Once a person becomes ajit, jujhar, and zorawar, then they naturally obtain fateh.

The eldest son of Guru Gobind Singh Ji, Baba Ajit Singh Ji, was 17 years young, when he gave his life in the struggle for justice. Guru Gobind Singh Ji's second son, Baba Jujhar Singh Ji was 13. Baba Zorawar Singh Ji was 9 years old, and Baba Fateh Singh Ji was 7. Mother Gujri Ji was 81 years old. Even though the sahibzaday were young in physical age, because of their great bravery and sacrifice, Sikhs refer to them as "Baba" (a term of reverence for saints and elderly men). Out of respect, the male Sikh heroes are referred to with the words "Baba" and "Bhai" (Brother). The female heroines are referred to as "Mother" or "Bibi" (mother/sister). It is important, as you read about their bravery and sacrifice, that you remember their ages.

This history, this journey of shahadat, this journey of bravery, love, and sacrifice, this is our journey. We are all travelers. As Sikhs, our life is meant to be spent following this journey. The road of this journey has been paved by those who walked before us, those who struggled so that our path would be easier than theirs. In return, we have a duty to continue the struggle so that we can make the path easier for those who come after us. This is the road of Guru Nanak Dev Ji. This is the road of Sikhi, which connects with our brothers, the beloved

Sahibzaday, and the heroic Gursikhs of today and tomorrow. This is the journey of Shahadat.

The Safar-E-Shahadat movement was started by Bhai Harpal Singh Ji, the Head Granthi of Gurudwara Fatehgarh Sahib, in 2013. Since December 2013, each year from 7-10 Poh (usually around December 22-26), Sikhs gather at the places where the younger sahibzaday and Mother Gujri Ji stayed during their journey and hold a smagam (religious service) in those same places. In this way, Sikhs walk the footsteps of the beloved Sahibzaday and Khalsa Panth. The four-day journey is as follows:

Day one (7 Poh): Gurudwara Chhann Baba Kuma Maskhi Ji (Village Chakk Dera, Ropar)

Day two (8 Poh): Gurudwara Attack Sahib (Village Saheri, Morinda)

Day three (9 Poh): Gurudwara Kotwali Sahib (Morinda)

Day four (10 Poh): Gurudwara Thanda Burj, Sri Fatehgarh Sahib (Sirhind)[15]

At each place, Bhai Harpal Singh Ji beautifully narrates the blessed history of each day, in a manner that pierces the hearts of all who listen.

---

[15] The city of Sirhind gets its name from two words, sir (head) and hind (India). During the Mughal rule, Sirhind was the resting point in between the two cities of Lahore and Delhi. It was believed that Lahore and Delhi were like arms and Sirhind was like the head of the Mughal rule.

This history provides a priceless roadmap for us travelers on this journey of Sikhi. This gathering inspires Sikhs to reconnect to their roots and remember their identity as the brave children of Guru Gobind Singh Ji, and the brothers and sisters of the four sahibzaday.

These four days are special time, where Sikhs around the world unite, as one family. On December 25, a day which is dark, cold, and barren in many countries, Christian brothers and sisters rejoice in Christ, and light Christmas lights to celebrate the birth of Jesus, who came as a light in the dark and frigid winter. Jewish brothers and sisters light their menorahs to celebrate liberation. African brothers and sisters celebrate the seven values of Kwanzaa. In these days which are significant for so many, Sikhs celebrate the actions of their ancestors who gave their lives to bring light and freedom to a dark and barren world.

On December 25, Sikhs commemorate "Dulay lohu dee vangaar, sada virsa sada parwar" meaning "The challenge of the spilled blood, our family, and our heritage." This is a day where Sikhs come together as family and contemplate whether we have risen to the challenge put forth by the spilled blood of our ancestors. Sikhs reflect on whether they have honored the legacy of the Gurus, the shaheeds, and the panth. During this season, as we see children around us excited for gifts and sweets, let us remember the bravery of sahibzaday. Let us remember how they faced torture and fought for freedom at the same age. As we see our children, snuggled warm, waiting for Santa Claus, let us feel

9

the pain that they willingly faced, hungry in the cold tower, so that the message of Gurbani could survive and reach us. When we see our children, and elderly parents, let us feel what Guru Gobind Singh Ji sacrificed for us. When we feed our children and protect them from the cold, let us remember the bitter cold that Mother Gujri Ji and the young sahibzaday suffered. Let us remember the cold darkness that the Khalsa army faced in the jungle, their clothes wet and torn, while crossing the Sirsa river. Let us remember that they suffered by choice. They suffered to keep the principles and ideology of Guru Nanak Dev Ji alive. They sacrificed so that revolutionary ideology could make this world better for us, and for the future generations after us.

This is a time to ask ourselves whether we have honored and valued the sacrifices and hard work of our ancestors. When a plant emerges from a seed, the seed breaks for the sake of the plant. The same way, our ancestors let their bodies die, for the sake of the plant of Sikhi, which grew in their hearts. It is up to the coming generations to water this plant, so it can become a tree that provides shade and comfort to the world.

Even though Sikhs watch the Safar-e-Shahadat smagam from different screens, in different countries and continents, it feels like we are all present together. The love of Guru Gobind Singh Ji connects us even from thousands of miles away. We are all one caravan, connected by our journey. This connection is the most powerful connection in the Universe. After the shahadat of the four beloved sahibzaday, Guru Gobind Singh Ji said, "It does not matter if I lost four children, thousands of my children still live on in my Sikhs. I will see the spirit of Baba Ajit Singh Ji, Baba Jujhar Singh Ji, Baba Zorawar Singh Ji, and Baba Fateh Singh Ji in my Khalsa." In 1704, Mother Gujri Ji sat here, where we sit today, with two of her beloved grandchildren. Today, millions of her beloved grandchildren sit here and remember her bravery.

It was the wish of Bhai Harpal Singh Ji that Sikhs never forget the brave sacrifices of Poh 1704. Sikhs should never forget their royal heritage and their mission of fighting cruelty and uplifting humanity. The history and lessons of Poh 1704 must be shared with the world. These lessons hold the power to save humankind from the despair that engulfs us today. They give our children the inspiration and strength to live a life of service with their heads held up high, even in the face of darkness and adversity. With Guru's grace, Bhai Harpal Singh Ji dreamed of starting this smagam, so that no matter where in the world a Sikh may be, their hearts will remain forever connected to Thanda Burj[16]. Bhai Harpal Singh Ji's relentless efforts have become fruitful. In the past 10 years, the Safar-e-Shahadat Smagam has been watched by millions of Sikhs worldwide. The path that Mother Gujri Ji and the Sahibzaday walked on has been renamed Safar-e-Shahadat Marg (way). Each month, similar smagams are held around the world,

---

[16] The cold tower where Mata Gujri Ji and the younger Sahibzaday were imprisoned. This book will describe the tower in more detail.

and they give strength to the worldwide Sikh diaspora.

This book is an English translation of the katha, the historical account of Poh 1704, as narrated by Bhai Harpal Singh Ji. One important aspect of this book is that this book's primary focus is not on what happened but on why it happened. There are multiple historical works which discuss the facts surrounding the sacrifices of Poh 1704. Most Sikhs know what happened during that time and have heard the historical facts many times However, it is not enough to know what happened, but also why it happened. Why did Guru Gobind Singh Ji sacrifice his family? Why did the Sikhs feel the need to stand against the government at the time? Why did the Khalsa take on a battle against a centuries old regime, when they were massively outnumbered? Why did they leave their homes and face freezing temperatures and starvation? What was the purpose of their sacrifices and what did the Khalsa wish to accomplish?

When we study what happened, we study the past. However, the sacrifices of the Sahibzaday and Sikhs are timeless. When we study the why, we are able to apply the lessons of the past to today. The same forces behind the circumstances which existed in 1704 continue to exist today. The Khalsa's struggle in 1704 is still the Khalsa's struggle now. The same evil that existed then, still exists now. As long as evil and cruelty remain on Earth, the Khalsa will remain fighting against it. It is only when we understand the reason behind the sacrifices made by our ancestors that we can wholeheartedly walk on this journey behind the Sahibzaday. Only then can we find the power to continue their mission.

The same principles which motivated the Sikhs in the past are the same values which Sikhs have a duty to fight for today. People die but mindsets don't. In this way, the same mindset lives on in different bodies. There are still many Gangus, Aurangzebs, and Wazir Khans today. The bodies may have changed, but the ideology is still alive. Their mindset of cruelty and tyranny lives on. Likewise, the mindset of Guru Nanak Dev Ji is also still alive in Gurbani and in the Sikhs.

The "deewar" (wall) is timeless, the "talwar" (sword) is timeless, and the "veechar" (ideology) is timeless. When Guru Nanak Dev Ji got married, those who feared Guru Ji's ideology tried to murder Guru Ji by causing a wall to collapse on top of him.[17] Likewise, the younger sahibzaday were sentenced to be executed by having a wall built around them, to suffocate them till death. These walls are symbolic. They are barriers to all-inclusive ideology of Guru Nanak Dev Ji, an ideology that united all of humanity. Walls are symbolic of division. They close things and make them smaller. Guru Nanak Dev Ji's ideology opened minds and hearts. The wall is also symbolic in Gurbani. Guru Granth Sahib Ji talks about the wall of falsehood that separates a human from truth and God called "koor da pal." Inside and

---

[17] Today, Gurudwara Kandh Sahib stands where this historic incident took place.

outside, a Sikh is always fighting to break barriers and tear down walls.

Today, when we practice the values of Guru Nanak Dev Ji, when we follow the veechar, the ideology, of Gurbani, we will also face deewars (walls). We will face those who want to build divisions. We will face narrow minded people who wish to limit Sikhi, and those who wish to spread hate. It is possible that these people will even look like Sikhs on the outside. The ideology of Guru Nanak Dev Ji will always remain a thorn for those who wish to spread darkness, exploit others, and keep people enslaved. The veechar of Guru Nanak Dev ji is timeless, the deewars are timeless, and the talwar, the battle of the Sikhs, is timeless. When we understand this, we realize that this is not their journey alone, it is our journey. It is our battle. In this way we do not just read about the Sahibzaday and the Gursikhs of the past, we connect to them. We truly become a part of Safar-e-Shahadat.

It is our hope that our blessed and unparalleled history can inspire Sikhs in English-speaking countries, especially those Sikhs who have been disconnected from their heritage. By learning about the bravery of their ancestors, they too can feel a sense of deep pride. Most of all, we wish that this translation will move readers to join our journey, to walk as children of Guru Gobind Singh Ji, to walk behind Baba Zorawar Singh Ji and Baba Fateh Singh Ji, and live their mission of banishing every trace of cruelty from the face of this Earth. That being said, we would like to now welcome you, the reader, to embark on this journey with us.

HISTORICAL BACKGROUND: THE JOURNEY FROM TALWANDI TO ANANDPUR SAHIB

A Lover is a Fighter

Guru Nanak Dev Ji revolutionized humanity's understanding of religion. He preached a path to God that transcended religious rituals and labels, a path which focused, first and foremost, on nurturing a loving connection to creation and the creator. Guru Nanak Dev Ji discarded all other forms of bhakti (devotion/worship) and preached that the highest form of worship is prema bhakti or the worship of love. There is no need to renounce the world, no need for penances, no need to fast, to wear certain clothing, or to go on pilgrimages. Guru Ji taught that we belong to God, we are part of God, and we can naturally connect to God through pure love. Love for God and creation is the ultimate worship.

According to Guru Granth Sahib, "bhakhiya bhaau apaar," is God's language.[18] The word "bhakhiya" means language, "bhaau" means love, and "apaar" means limitless. The language of unlimited love is the universal language of God. It is a language that anyone can speak. All beings are born speaking this language, but they forget it. A person cannot communicate with God until they relearn this language. Anyone can experience God by breaking the barriers of the heart and loving all without boundaries. This love is how one communicates with God. Anyone from any religion can speak this language. The deaf, blind, and mute can speak it. Humans can speak it. Animals and plants can speak it. Without speaking this language, one cannot connect to God, no matter which religious ritual they may perform.

After Guru Nanak Dev Ji, the nine following Gurus not only envisioned a world ruled by compassion, but also took

---

[18] Guru Granth Sahib Ji, 2

17

practical steps to implement this vision. They built systems and institutions to ensure that the needs of all of God's children are taken care of. They constructed Gurudwaras[19] (Sikh places of worship) in every village they visited. These Gurudwaras exemplified prema bhakti. All Gurudwaras included large community kitchens which served free meals to all (langars), hospitals, schools, shelters, fitness arenas (the equivalent of modern-day gyms), large gardens, and even animal sanctuaries. All these things were available free of charge. The Gurus dug wells and built sarovars[20] (water tanks for bathing), so that everyone had access to clean water. In this way each person's core needs were taken care of for free, unconditionally. The Gurus believed that no human should have to starve or lack basic human dignities. Everyone should have access to clean drinking water, education, and medical care. These are absolute rights. No one should have to worry about these necessities.

The concept of seva (selfless service) still lives on in the Sikhs of today. Gurdwaras still serve free food to millions of people daily in langars which are open 24/7. They still provide shelter to all, and many Gurudwaras still have sarovars. During the Coronavirus Pandemic, when food was scarce and overpriced, Sikhs brought langar to remote villages. When even the government of India ran low on oxygen, and people were selling it for ridiculous amounts of money, Sikhs built hospitals and gave out oxygen cylinders for free, calling it the langar of oxygen. The efforts of the Gurudwara were recognized by governments worldwide.

---

[19] Called Dharmshalas at time. Guru Granth Sahib teaches that this whole earth is God's Dharamshala. Each Sikh home is also a Dharamshala.

[20] The institution of langar and the building of sarovars were also steps to spread equality and destroy the Caste System. People would eat their meals sitting together and bathe in the same water, thus undermining Caste-based segregation.

After every calamity or natural disaster, the Khalsa army is always ready to serve. Each Sikh dreams and works towards upholding the Gurudwara system designed by the Gurus and creating a world where no one has to live without basic human dignities.

Not only did the Gurudwara ensure that the physical and spiritual needs of all people were met, the concept of "sangat," insured that everyone's mental health needs were also taken care of. Sangat refers to a gathering of Sikhs. This word is deeply rooted in the concept of community. The role of sangat is especially important in light of the current mental health crisis. Guru Granth Sahib Ji describes the concept of sangat by saying "I have forgotten all animosity ever since I joined the holy sangat, here no one is an enemy, and no one is a stranger. Here, I have come to understand that we all belong to each other."[21] The literal meaning of the word "sangat" is companionship. The "sadh sangat" (holy sangat) is founded on the belief that we are all souls on a journey. For the lone traveler, it is easy to get lost or lose hope on the way. Sadh sangat is a caravan, where souls come together and support each other in this journey of life.

Today, many people feel lonely. Sadh sangat is the cure for that loneliness. It is a place of pure love and acceptance. Everyone sits, prays, and eats together as the family of God, as equals, regardless of social status. This concept was and still is revolutionary. The creation of sadh sangat ensured that no one ever felt alone. Strangers became family and thieves became saints, upon meeting the guru's sadh sangat. The love found in sangat infused strength into the Sikhs. This love is still the biggest asset of the Khalsa Panth. The Guru's recognized that just as food is important to sustain the body, and Gurbani is important to nourish the

---

[21] Guru Granth Sahib Ji, 1299

soul, sadh sangat is crucial for a person's mental wellbeing. The company we keep effects our destiny. That is why holy company is so important. As society becomes more isolated, it is important that sangat remains a judgement free place where all are welcomed and embraced.

The love a true Sikh has for humanity is so strong that a Sikh would even lay down their lives to protect those in peril. Sikhs don't live for themselves; they live for the Creator and creation. Traditionally, Sikh homes were run like Gurudwaras, and were open to those who needed food and shelter. Historical sources describe the way Sikhs shared meals by saying:

"After preparing the meal, the Sikh calls out "is anyone hungry?" During that time even enemies are welcome to eat, and they are embraced as friends. The Sikh serves others first and only eats after everyone else is satisfied. They treat each other like family and give each other deep respect. They have such an honorable tradition; they give their lives for each other and love each other even more than they love their own breath. "22

Lovingly serving creation is the way of worship for a Sikh. Making this world a kinder and more loving place is the mission of each Sikh and the very root of the Sikh faith.

---

22 These historical words stem from a conversation between Nadir Shah and Ahmed Shab Abdali, rulers who wanted to eliminate Sikhs. Nadir Shah asked Abdali how the Sikhs were so powerful while being so small in number. The Punjabi version of this starts as "Dayt awaja bhukha koe, Deg tiar Guru Ki Hoye." These historical words are still widely quoted today, and some Sikhs say these words before their meals.

Not a Single Moghul Soldier Turned Blind.

When you love someone, you do all you can to alleviate their suffering. A true saint loves all of creation because creation is dear to God. In order to love God, you must love God's children. Naturally, when you love someone, you can't bear their pain. In this way, a true saint cannot bear the pain of creation. A real saint does not stay silent when others are being hurt. The Gurus taught that when innocent people suffer Sikhs have a duty to stand up and fight for them.

When Emperor Babar brutally attacked India, committing genocide, Guru Nanak Dev Ji asked where all the Saints were? Why were they silent when humanity was suffering? This is where the Sikh principle of "miri and piri" started. The word "miri" means worldly power. A mir is a person of the world, or a person that has obtained worldly success. The highest forms of mirs would have been kings. "Piri" means spiritual power. A pir is someone who has obtained spiritual success. The highest forms of pirs would have been saints. Miri is the truth of power and piri is the power of truth.

Traditionally, miri and piri were seen as opposites. Prior to Guru Nanak Dev Jis time, the Indian tradition was that a person either shunned worldliness and pursued spirituality or pursued worldliness. It was unheard of pursue both. Saints were expected to leave their families and meditate in caves, forests, and basements. They usually remained celibate or left their houses behind to live in isolation. A saint had no buisness meddling in the affairs of the world.

Guru Nanak Dev Ji flipped this concept by combining miri and piri and putting worldly power into the hands of good people. Guru Ji preached that shunning the world and leaving humanity to suffer was selfishness disguised as worship. Guru Nanak Dev Ji taught that the live of a householder was beautiful and one did not have to leave that life to find God. Guru Ji encouraged saints to leave their isolation and actively fight for social justice. By giving the pirs the power of miri, worldly power stayed in the hands of those who would use that power for good.

When Emperor Babar invaded India, people prayed to their saints (pirs) to save them, yet these pirs were helpless in the face of Babar (the mir). The victims of Babar's attacks believed that the pirs would pray and perform miracles. They believed the saints would read mantras that would cause Babar and his soldiers to go blind. The innocent people relied on this belief to their detriment. They died waiting for the spells of the pirs to save them. Guru Nanak Dev Ji said that instead of chanting spells, the pirs should be out there standing up to Babar.

Guru Nanak Dev Ji wrote about the torture, rape, and bloodshed which took place during Babar's genocide. Victims thought that if they pray to their pirs, the pirs will meditate and put a spell on the soldiers and make them blind. Their hopes were shattered as they were attacked and their prayers to the pirs remained unanswered. Guru Nanak Dev Ji describes their disappointment by saying "Not a single Moghul soldier turned blind and there were no miracles."[23]

Instead of ignoring the cries of those around him, instead of closing his eyes and meditating, Guru Nanak Dev Ji stood up to Babar and called him a tyrant to his face. Guru Nanak Dev Ji was even arrested by Babar's forces and imprisoned. When brought before Babar, Guru Nanak Dev

---

[23] Guru Granth Sahib Ji, 417

Ji called for the release of all those Babar had incarcerated. Guru Ji enlightened Babar and spoke the fierce truth to his heart. From this day onwards, it was understood that all Sikhs have a duty, a duty born from compassion, to stand up when God's children are being hurt.

Sikhi teaches that while it is a sin to engage in cruelty, it is a bigger sin to tolerate it. Guru Nanak Dev Ji's path is of proactive compassion. The soul is purified by meditating on God, and the body is purified by helping the meek. Both spiritual strength and spiritual courage are needed. If praying alone was enough, then what was the need for humans to have bodies? We could have been born with souls alone, since praying requires just a soul and not a body. It is not enough to live a life of passive worship.

Guru Nanak Dev Ji laid the foundation Sikhs to live as warrior-saints. Guru Nanak Dev Ji was already connected to God. He did not have to leave his family and his comfortable life behind. Guru Nanak Dev Ji had every material comfort. By choosing to travel to the most dangerous places and put his life in risk to uplift humanity, Guru Nanak Dev Ji showed us love in action.

Defining "Shahadat": When Love Shatters the Limits of our Body

Guru Nanak Dev Ji taught that love is not merely something you feel, and not even merely something you do, it is something you become. Shahadat is the highest point of love. To lose oneself and become love is shahadat. Guru Nanak Dev Ji wrote "If you wish to play the game of love, then come down my path with your head in the palm of your hand."[24] Placing your head in your hand means you are

---

[24] Guru Granth Sahib Ji, 1410

surrendering yourself to love. You have let go of your thoughts, ego, and identity. According to Guru Nanak Dev Ji, this is the only way to love God. Love must not merely touch you, but it must engulf you completely. Love has no limits. A person does not control love. Love controls the person. Gurbani teaches "to find God, you must lose yourself, there is no other trick."[25]

The love that Gurbani refers to is not a worldly love. It is a love that can only be experienced by those who have connected to God within themselves. In today's world this connection is rare because humans have turned religion into outward rituals and lost sight of the real purpose of worship. The real purpose of worship is not to fulfill a formality, or merely ask God for things. It is to connect with our creator.

While many people meditate, this meditation is often used for focus or to calm the mind, but it is rarely used as a way to lovingly connect to the Creator. Gurbani says the state of one who is connected to God is beyond all description. It is a state which cannot be understood by anyone except for the one who has reached it. It is a bliss beyond all bliss. It is a love so strong that nothing else matters, not even the fear of death.

It is only by reaching this state that one can become a true warrior or a "shaheed" (one who reaches shahadat). This state of love is described by Bhai Gurdas Ji[26], the primary Sikh historian, as a state where one lives in God's love and

---

[25] Guru Granth Sahib Ji, 722

[26] Bhai Gurdas Ji (1551-circa 1637)- Bhai Gurdas Ji was a Sikh scholar during the time period of Guru Amar Das Ji (third Guru of the Sikhs) until the time period of Guru Har Gobind Sahib Ji (sixth Guru of the Sikhs). Bhai Gudas Ji was the scribe of the Sikhs during that time and Guru Arjun Dev Ji (fifth Guru of the Sikhs) referred to his writings as the key for understanding Gurbani.

becomes dead to the darkness of this world. A shaheed overcomes their desires. Shahadat is a state that one must experience, a state that is not reached by mere words. A shaheed embraces endless forbearance and deep faith. They are always ready to serve. A shaheed is beyond pain and pleasure, beyond crying and laughter. Sikhi has a history of martyrs who lovingly and happily gave their lives in service of humanity. In order to become a shaheed, one must die inwardly before their body faces death.[27] They must rise above fear and greed.

According to Gurbani, the body does not have to die for a person to experience the afterlife. The body is a mere cloth. Just like humans change their clothes, the soul changes its body. The existence of the soul is infinite. When a person dies, their soul does not change in any other way besides shedding the body. If a soul connects with God during the life of the body, then the soul will continue towards God even after the body dies. If the soul has not connected with God, it will continue onwards on its beautiful journey towards obtaining this connection, sometimes taking different bodies and lifeforms, each with unique lessons.

Life is a journey of the soul and not the body. The soul does not take birth when a body is born. The soul is as old as God. It is been around forever. The soul does not die, when the body dies. It moves onwards on its separate and unique journey. Sometimes, someone who has already found God still reincarnates and comes back in the world. They come to serve as guides for others. Gurbani talks about such souls saying, *"They are not stuck in the cycle of life and death,*

---

[27] "Murda hoye mureed, na galee howana"- Vaaran Bhai Gurdas Ji,3, Pauri 18

God's servants come to uplift others. "[28] Such souls are rare, and they have a natural spiritual connection and inclination. Every human has the ability to witness and experience God through prema bhakti. In this way they obtain salvation while alive. Gurbani calls this the state of becoming "jeevan mukat" or liberated while alive. To be "mukat" is to be free. It is freedom from vices and fear. One is jeevan mukat when they no longer fear death. Only one who is jeevan mukat can become a shaheed.

In addition to losing the fear of death, another necessary character trait of a shaheed is not having any worldly greed. One who is greedy for material things will not be able to become a shaheed. Even the greed to live will keep someone from following the path of shahadat. Many times, Sikhs were offered riches in exchange for compliance with cruelty. If a Sikh agreed to renounce their faith, or renounce their struggle, that Sikhs life would be spared from torture and execution. Still Sikhs gave their life over and over. Of the thousands of Sikhs captured by the government, not one surrendered. Many times, standing up to cruelty is akin to writing your own death warrant. It is not easy to fight against those who have power. A person who is cowardly or greedy will give up his fight due to the fear of death or in exchange for material things. Only those who have defeated fear and greed can reach shahadat.

Like defeating fear, defeating greed is also accomplished by experiencing God within. Gurbani teaches that the happiness of experiencing God is greater than any material joy. The state of endless bliss experienced through God realization is called "Anand." Material joys are temporary and lead to ennui. Even kings with unmatched material

---

[28] "Janam maran do mein nahi, jan parupkaree aiye" – Guru Granth Sahib Jee, 748

wealth have not found happiness. Only those who are connected with God can reach Anand. Those who know the happiness of Anand no longer thirst for worldly pleasures. Food, drinks, wealth, lust, and worldly love may give pleasure, but those pleasures are often short lived. The pleasure of Anand is infinite and never becomes dull or boring.

It is human nature to have some desires which change as a person grows and matures. When babies are born, they want milk. An infant will cry out for milk. Later, as the infant grows and is able to enjoy a variety of food, the child's strong desires for milk decrease. A child no longer wants milk all hours of the day. Instead, they want things like chocolates, cake, pizza, and candies. A young child often cries when their toy is broken. Later, when they become an adult and experience all the joys that money can buy, they no longer cry over broken toys. As adults make more money, their standards of enjoyment increase. The things they may not have been able to have as children now become a normal part of life. Their desires become bigger. A newly independent youth is excited when they buy their first apartment. Then they have their first home, and the joy of having an apartment is not like it was when they first became independent. The desire for a bicycle turns into the desire for a car. In this way, as humans experience bigger things, smaller things lose their importance. Anand is the biggest pleasure which makes all other happiness lose its value. In comparison to the experience of Anand, all other pleasures are dim. One who experiences Anand gets addicted to that experience. Anand is so powerful that it takes away the burning thirst in a human's heart.

Both fear and greed are overcome the same way, with "anbhav". Anbhav means knowledge gained by practical experience, in contrast to theory. Guru Granth Sahib Ji teaches, "Where there is anbhav, there is no fear. Where there is fear, there is no God (one does not realize God)."[29] One can obtain knowledge about God, through reading scripture, however, this knowledge is secondary. It is not anbhav. Anbhav is the experience of God, not just the knowledge of God. Until one experiences God firsthand, there are still doubts in their mind. In order to die while alive, anbhav is necessary. Anbhav leads a person to Anand. Anbhav is beyond religion. Anyone from any faith who loves God can get the same anbhav. All the saints whose writings are in Guru Granth Sahib Ji were from different faiths, yet they all had the same anbhav of God. God cannot be defined, only experienced. One who has experienced God, who has found Anand through anbhav, that person alone is free from fear and greed. That person alone can become a shaheed.

The First Accounts of Shahadat in Sikh History

The very first shaheed was a Muslim devotee of Guru Nanak Dev Ji, Qazi Rukn Ud-Din from Baghdad.[30] He fell in love with the message of Guru Nanak Dev Ji. The priests of that time could not see beyond religious labels, and they shunned Quazi Rukn Ud-Din for following a Guru who was non-Muslim. Quazi Rukn Ud-Din was called an infidel and the Mullahs (priests) in Mecca, Saudi Arabia issued decrees (fatwas) against him. These fatwas included (1) declaring that Qazi Rukn Ud-din is a kafir (infidel) because he

---

[29] "Jeh anbhau toh bhai nahi, jeh bhau toh har nahi"- Guru Granth Sahib Ji, 1374

[30] Siyahto Baba Nanak Fakir: Taajudin's Diary- Account of a Muslim author who accompanied Guru Nanak Dev Ji from Mecca to Baghdad- Syyed Pritpal Singh

followed Guru Nanak Dev Ji, who they said was "a kafir whose teachings are blasphemous" (2) confiscating all of Qazi Rukn Ud-din's property (3)ordering his kin to leave the country (4) giving him thirty lashes (5) locking him in a dark box without food for eleven days (6) painting his face black and parading him through the streets of Mecca mounted on a camel (7) hanging him upside down (8) burying him in hot sand, and (9) executing him by burying him up to his neck in sand and throwing stones at him until he died. Qazi Rukn Ud- Din had already experienced God. He had felt anbhav. He had reached Anand. His heart was connected to the ultimate reality. His greatest love was God. For this reason, he did not fear death. He did not fear losing his riches. Qazi Rukn Ud-Din welcomed death with a smiling face. When it was time for two men to record his last words, as was done according to Sharia law when a person was executed, Qazi Rukn Ud- Deen, loudly proclaimed his love for Guru Nanak Dev Ji.

The second shaheed was a five-year-old child, named Bhai Tara Popat.[31] He was martyred when Emperor Babar attacked India in 1526. During this time, the army of King Babar had lit houses on fire and was burning people to death. Bhai Tara Popat started cupping his small hands, filling them with water, and throwing the water on the fires in order to put them out. Babar's soldiers laughed at the child. They asked Bhai Tara Popat if he really believed that his small five-year-old hands could put out any fire. Bhai Tara Popat said that it did not matter whether he was able to put out the fire, all that mattered is that he, a Sikh of Guru Nanak Dev Ji, was not on the side of those lighting the fire, nor was he a silent bystander. He was actively fighting on the side of

---

[31] *Singh, Kharak (1997). "Martyrdom in Sikhism". Sikhism, Its Philosophy & History. Chandigarh: Institute of Sikh Studies: 18.*

goodness by trying his best to put out the fires. Upon hearing his answer, the soldiers threatened to kill Bhai Tara Popat if he did not stop. Bhai Tara Popat continued to put out the fires and the soldiers ended up throwing him into one of the fires, where he became a shaheed.

Guru Arjun Dev Ji was the first Sikh Guru to become a shaheed. He was seen as a threat to the government because he was making people fearless by connecting them with God. During this time, the majority of people in Punjab were either those who worshipped idols or those who worshipped the graves of Muslim mystics (called "kabar pujak"). The largest following was that of a mystic called "Sakhee Sarvar". While worshiping graves is considered taboo in Islam, since the grave was of a Muslim saint, this was seen as a way by the government to bring people into the fold of their version of Islam. Those who previously worshiped graves were inspired by the teachings of Guru Arun Dev Ji. They started flocking towards Guru Arjun Dev Ji and they adopted the teachings of Gurbani. Guru Arjun Dev Ji united both Hindus and Muslims with the universal message of Gurbani. This was problematic for the government, who were threatened by Guru Jis following.

Punjab is divided into three regions, Majha, Malwa, and Doaba. In each region, there was one leader for all the grave worshippers. This leader was called a Bharai. The Bharai of Majha was named Bhai Langah Ji, the Bharai of Malwa was named Bhai Peloh Ji, and the Bharai of Doaba was named Bhai Manjh Ji. All three of these leaders were inspired by Guru Arjun Dev Ji and became Sikhs. They stopped worshiping graves and encouraged their followers to do the same. They even uprooted the graves they once worshipped. This is a sign of mental strength. They uprooted what they once feared. This is an example about how direct connection to God makes one fearless. Guru Arjun Dev Ji's influence worried the government. If people no longer feared the graves they once worshipped and bowed before, it was a matter of time until they no longer feared the leaders.

Naturally, priests and leaders, who wish to control the public, would be threatened when people no longer remained afraid of them. This was in a society where people were split into castes, and lower castes were supposed to be subservient to higher castes. It was a time period where kings ruled by fear and a low caste person was not allowed to even hear prayers or enter temples. Guru Arjun Dev Ji connected these so called "low castes" with God and told them that they were equal to everyone else and not be afraid of anyone.

When Guru Arjun Dev Ji complied Guru Granth Sahib Ji and added the writings of the Gurus and saints before him, it caused unprecedented social upheaval. In addition to the first four Gurus, Guru Granth Sahib Ji contained the writings of Muslims, and so called "low caste" saints like Bhagat Namdev Ji, who was thrown out of a mandir (Hindu temple) because of his caste, saints like Bhagat Ravidas Ji, who belonged to the lowest caste, a chamar, whose body and even shadow was considered inauspicious. Guru Arjun Dev Ji included their writings in Gurbani, and people of all castes worshipped them. Muslims and Hindus alike came and gave their respects. People became fearless and stopped tolerating cruelty, even from the government. They had the courage to challenge centuries old institutions such as the caste system. Guru Arjun Dev Ji freed the public from this age-old institution. This terrified the oppressors. If people could challenge beliefs that were set in stone for centuries, they could easily challenge the power of the government.

Guru Arjun Dev Ji was given a choice, he could either pay a small fine, erase the hymns from Guru Granth Sahib Ji which the government disagreed with, and convert to Islam, or he could face a torturous death. Guru Arjun Dev Ji could have easily paid the fine, he had the money readily available. It was a matter of not bowing down before cruelty. Guru Ji had no problem with people from any religion and fought for the freedom of Hindus and Muslims to worship as they wish. Likewise, Jahangir didn't really want to execute Guru Arjun Dev Ji. Instead, he wanted to bring him under his control and to make him subservient. Even today, leaders use priests to win over public influence. Guru Arjun Dev Ji refused to pay the fine or erase the hymns of Guru Granth Sahib Ji. He refused to be used by the leaders to control the public. Therefore, Guru Arjun Dev Ji was sentenced to be executed under *Yassa*. Under *Yassa*, Guru Ji's execution would excessively painful and not a drop of blood was allowed to drop under the ground. The government tried to defame Guru Arjun Dev Ji and hurt his spirit, however, these attempts were to no avail.

Guru Arjun Dev Ji happily welcomed this torture and execution. He was forced to sit on top of a burning stove for five days. Guru Arjun Dev Ji was starved and kept thirsty the whole time. Burning sand was poured on his head. During this torture, Guru Ji lovingly sang, "Dear God, your will is so sweet to me." In this way, Guru Ji showed all the Sikhs the path of a warrior. Before this, there had been many accounts of saints who had faced torture and prayed to God for miracles. However, this was different. Instead of praying to be saved, Guru Arjan Dev Ji showed what it means to be strong and blissful even during the darkest times.

Tyrants Should Sit at the Foot of your Bed

After the martyrdom of Guru Arjun Dev Ji, the Sikhs fought many battles. This was a turning point in history.

Prior to the time of Emperor Jahangir, the government had mostly accepted pluralism. During Jahangir's time, this started to change. The government became increasingly cruel, and Sikhs stood up against this cruelty. There were many saheeheds during the battles which took place in the time of Guru Hargobind Sahib Ji and Guru Har Rai Sahib Ji (sixth and seventh Sikh Gurus). Guru Hargobind Sahib Ji established the Akal Thakat, the timeless throne, as the seat of authority for all Sikhs. At one point Guru Hargobind Sahib Ji did forgive Emperor Jahangir, and even saved his life. However, a rift between the Sikhs and the government started to form during the rise of Aurangzeb, a totalitarian ruler who believed in Islamic fanaticism. Guru Har Rai Ji and Guru Har Krishan Ji refused to meet with Aurangzeb because of his cruelty and intolerance.

In order to usurp the throne, Aurangzeb murdered his brother, Dara Shikoh, and incarcerated his father, Shah Jahan. Dara Shikoh was very saintly and was very close to Guru Har Rai Ji. As a child, Dara Shikoh was once very sick. He was taken to every hospital yet the only place he found a cure was in the free medical dispensary of Guru Har Rai Sahib. In his quest for the throne, Aurangzeb chopped off Dara Shikoh's head and sent it to their father, on the day of Eid, which is a holy time of grace and mercy for Muslims.[32] Aurangzeb also executed a saint named Sarmad Fakeer, who was a friend of Dara Shikoh, and had stood up to Aurangzeb. This Saint, like Dara Shikoh, was also close to Guru Har Rai Ji.

---

[32] This shows how much those who use religion as a pretext really care about their faith. It is an act of utmost disrespect to commit such an action on such a holy day. Anyone who truly was a good Muslim would never disrespect the day of Eid in this manner.

Aurangzeb's policies became increasingly cruel and intolerant. For this reason, Sikhs started to protest the government. When Guru Gobind Singh Ji (whose name was still Gobind Rai at the time) was around five years old, the Nawab (a position much like a governor or viceroy) of Patna Sahib was passing through the place where Guru Gobind Singh Ji was gathered with friends of his age. The Nawab was surrounded by his officers and one officer instructed the children to bow down in respect of the Nawab. Guru Gobind Singh Ji refused to bow down in protest of Aurangzeb's cruelty. Instead, Guru Gobind Singh Ji and his friends made faces at the Nawab and his procession. This was very dangerous, and it is likely that the reason the children's lives were spared was due to their age. Aurangzeb had already executed others who mocked and criticized his regime.

Word of this incident spread fast, and Guru Teg Bahadur Ji (ninth Sikh Guru and father of Guru Gobind Singh Ji) [33] issued a hukamnama[34] regarding the incident. In this hukamnama, Guru Teg Bahadur Ji praised Guru Gobind Singh Ji's refusal to bow down and his protest of cruelty. The hukamnama read:

"That which Gobind Rai did, it was very good. He did the right thing. One should always keep tyrants at the feet of your bed (pendi) and never at the head (sirandi)."

Traditionally, when seating someone with respect, or when someone has a high status, a host would have them sit on the side of the bed where the head goes (called sirandi). The host would sit at the foot of the bed (pendi). This is a sign of subservience and humility. If a high government official, or an elder, or anyone in a position of power would

---

[33] Ninth Sikh Guru, Father of Guru Gobind Singh Ji, see pg. 30
[34] Decree

come visit, they were seated at the head of the bed. Here, Guru Teg Bahadur Ji is saying that one should never blindly bow towards those in power.

Here, as a father, Guru Teg Bahadur Ji is telling his son, and all Sikhs, there is no need to allow those in power to control your every action. There is no reason to feel small in front of them, or to fear them. Gurbani teaches that a king or ruler is a *"mard ka chela"*[35] a devotee, or a servant, of their people. A leader should always be humble and willing to serve. Gurbani says that those in power are answerable to their subjects. A citizen should always be awake, supervising their leaders, like an employer supervises the work of their employee. A Sikh is always an aware citizen. This level of human dignity and confidence preached by the Sikh Gurus was revolutionary, and it awakened self-respect in a population that was used to living with their heads bowed low.

Giving your Life to Protect what you Don't Believe in.

Aurangzeb's intolerance led to further oppression and forced conversions. During this time, there was a campaign to force Hindus to convert to Islam. Many Hindus were forced to remove their religious symbols including the Hindu sacred thread ("Janeu"). Sikhi disagrees with the wearing of the Janeu and Gurbani preaches strongly against it. Ironically, even though Guru Teg Bahadur Ji was against wearing the janeu, today Guru Teg Bahadur Ji is known as the "protector of the Janeu." This is because Guru Teg Bahadur Ji strongly believed in freedom of religion and human rights, and even gave his life to defend this freedom.

---

[35] Guru Granth Sahib Ji, 722

When Guru Gobind Singh Ji was 9 years old, a group of Kashmiri Hindu Priests, led by Priest Kirpa Ram, came to see Guru Teg Bahadur Ji and to tell Guru Teg Bahadur Ji of their pain. They did not want to leave their religion and sought Guru Teg Bahadur Ji's help and intervention. Young Guru Gobind Singh Ji told his father that he must go and defend their rights, even if it would mean giving up his own life. Guru Teg Bahadur Ji stood up for the Hindu priests like their shield. Guru Ji told Aurangzeb, that if he was able to convert him then all the priests will convert. However, if Aurangzeb failed to convert Guru Teg Bahadur Ji then he must stop forcing others to convert.

Aurangzeb tried relentlessly to convert Guru Teg Bahadur Ji. Guru Ji was kept in a steel cage, where he could neither sit down nor stand up straight. He was not given food for over a month. Three of Guru Teg Bahadur Ji's close Sikhs, Bhai Mati Das Ji, Bhai Sati Das Ji, and Bhai Dayala Ji, were tortured and killed in front of Guru Ji, in an effort to scare Guru Ji and break his resolve. All three Sikhs were given the option to convert or face death. Bhai Mati Das Ji was to be executed by being sawed in half. He happily accepted this punishment and said it was a blessing because his life would be sacrificed in the struggle of humanity.

The word for saw in Punjabi is "ara." Bhai Mati Das Ji referred to the saw that was used to execute him as "piara," or beloved. His last wish was to be executed while facing his dear Guru, the guru who taught him to live in service, love beyond all limits, and not fear death. Bhai Sati Das Ji also chose execution. His body was wrapped in cotton and burnt alive. Bhai Dayala Ji was boiled alive in a burning cauldron. All three Sikhs kept theirs faces turned toward Guru Teg Bahadur Ji and happily gave their lives for human rights and religious freedom.

After so many efforts, Aurangzeb was not able to break the resolve of Guru Teg Bahadur Ji. Guru Ji was ordered to be executed. Guru Teg Bahadur Ji was to be beheaded in the middle of Chandi Chowk, a busy city square of Delhi. An executioner named Jalal ud Din, from a town called Samana, would behead Guru Teg Bahadur Ji. Jalal ud Din was the son of Noor ud Din, the executioner who executed Guru Arjan Dev Ji (who was the paternal Grandfather of Guru Teg Bahadur Ji). Guru Teg Bahadur Ji Ji prayed the Jap Ji Sahib and bowed his blessed head down in respect of Gurbani. Guru Ji's beautiful head was chopped right as he was bowing, as if to surrender it to God. The blessed head which refused to bow before in the face of hunger, torture, and death now bowed to the almighty Waheguru. A King who claimed to serve Allah, mercilessly tortured and murdered Allah's beloved saint. With this sacrifice, Guru Teg Bahadur Ji became the first martyr in the world to give his life, in the name of human rights, for an idea he disagreed with.

The Army of Compassion and the City of Bliss.

Prior to his shahadat, Guru Teg Bahadur Ji wrote the prayer "Salok Mahalla Nauvan." This prayer is full of wisdom, and it is a beacon to all about the realities of life and death. The last verse of this prayer describes the infinite inner strength that comes from surrendering to God and contains the following couplet. This couplet, reads:

"My strength is gone, chains are on my body, I cannot do anything or make any effort. In this helplessness, it is God alone who can support me, like he saved the devotee Gaj."

"I have been filled with great strength, my chains have been broken, I can do everything, make every effort, nothing is

impossible for me. Oh Nanak, everything is your hands God, you will be there to support me." [36]

This couplet embodies the Sikh spirit of chardikala, of endless optimism and positivity, which is rooted in the deep faith that God will always do good. The first part of this line and the second part are exact opposites and show how faith in God gives great strength in hopelessness and brings the impossible within reach.

After Guru Teg Bahadur Ji was executed, Aurangzeb forbade anyone to pick up Guru Ji's body and decapacitated head. Anyone who did so would be punished. Aurangzeb wanted to disrespect Guru Ji's body and use it to scare the public into obedience. However, that night there was a fierce storm. Seeing this opportunity, Sikhs captured the blessed body and decapacitated head of Guru Ji. The blessed body of the Guru was taken care of and cremated by a Sikh named Bhai Lakhi Shah Vanjara. In order to be inconspicuous, Bhai Lakhi Shah Ji respectfully cremated Guru Teg Bahadur Ji's body by burning down his whole house, including all his wealth, with Guru Ji's body still in it. That way people would think that Bhai Lakhi Shah Ji's house caught fire. Otherwise, neighbors would ask why the cremation was taking place. Bhai Lakhi Shah Ji was very wealthy, he was a merchant with many carts (he would be considered a billionaire by today's terms), and he sacrificed all his wealth to give Guru Ji a proper cremation. As his house burned, Bhai Lakhi Shah circled around it, a practice called parkarma, which is done out of respect. People thought that Bhai Lakhi Shah had become so distraught at the sight of his house on fire, that he was pacing around in circles. In reality, he was showing respect to Guru Teg Bahadur Ji during the cremation.

---

[36] Guru Granth Sahib Ji,

A Sikh named Bhai Jaita Ji brought Guru Teg Bahadur Ji's decapacitated head back to 9-year-old Guru Gobind Singh Ji, who was at Anandpur Sahib. Anandpur Sahib or the "city of bliss," was founded by Guru Teg Bahadur Ji. It had been a ghost town for many years, but Guru Teg Bahadur Ji turned it into a beautiful city. It is said that the same way this barren town turned into the city of bliss with Guru Ji's touch, the touch of Gurbani turns our barren hearts into oceans of love.

When Guru Gobind Singh Ji saw his beloved father's head, he did not scream or show fear. Instead, he embraced Bhai Jaita Jee, said that he is the precious child of the guru[37], and told the Sikhs to thank God that his father made his lifetime valuable by giving his life fighting for others. Guru Gobind Singh Ji writes about his father's bravery in *Bachitar Nanak*. This principle of standing up for the beliefs of others, despite their faith, is a core part of Sikhi. The Sikh tradition of standing up to tyranny developed into a legacy which was perfected with the creation of the Khalsa. A true Khalsa is ready to lay down their lives fighting anywhere that there is suffering. They never turn down those in need and see serving humanity as serving God.

In order to become a Khalsa, a person must partake in "Amrit", the Sikh baptism. The word "Amrit" means beyond death, or immortal. To prepare Amrit, Sikh prayers are read around a vessel of water. This holy water is mixed with a kirpan[38] and sugar is added to the mixture. This symbolizes that a Sikh should be sweet but also brave. All Sikhs, drink from the same vessel. This is to symbolize

---

[37] *Rangreta Guru Ka Beta*-Historical phrase, this was the title given to Bhai Jaita Ji, whose last name was Rangreta.

[38] A Kirpan is a holy sword. The word "kirpan" is made up of two words, "kirpa" or "mercy," and "aan," or "human dignity." This represents a Sikhs duty to fight for compassion and dignity for all.

equality and unity. It was unheard of, prior to this, for someone from a low caste to drink from the same vessel as someone of a high caste. Caste based segregation was and still is quite prevalent in India. A low caste person could be put to death even if their shadow passed by a priest who was engaged in prayer. Drinking from the same vessel was unimaginable. Once a Sikh takes Amrit, it symbolizes rebirth as a Khalsa. A person's prior caste, lineage, and beliefs are all history. From now on, the Khalsa lives their life as a saint soldier. They vow to never refrain from doing the right thing, even if it means risking their lives.

Anandpur Sahib is considered the family home of the Khalsa. Sikh hearts will always remain attached to Anandpur Sahib. When a Sikh takes Amrit, they are told from now on your spiritual home and birthplace is Anandpur Sahib. At Anandpur Sahib, Guru Gobind Singh Ji gathered warriors, poets, the best scholars, and even comedians to teach the sangat. Guru Gobind Singh Ji had a reputation for respecting scholars. Guru Ji would gift the scholars and artists who visited Anandpur Sahib horses and elephants, which were considered highly valuable at the time. One time, a scholar was given so many horses and elephants that when he left back with them people thought there was a stampede. Guru Gobind Singh Ji invited scholars and artists from all fields and religions. These artists included gardeners and painters. People came from far and wide to visit or reside in Anandpur Sahib. Everyone had access to the best free education. This led to an all-around enlightened environment. There was love in all directions. The Sikhs lived as a family. The sangat served all. Everyday new people would come, and Guru Gobind Singh Ji would lead them on the path to truth. Those who were lost in despair found a family. Those who were lonely were cared for and welcomed.

There are many interesting historical sakhis (true stories) of the marvelous and interesting events which took place at Anandpur Sahib. Each day, there was joy and pure love. There was no hunger or hatred, no jealousy or crime. Everyone had enough and shared with others. Everyone lived in harmony with God and nature. The lonely and downtrodden found love and shelter. It truly was the city of bliss and remains the perfect roadmap for how Sikh communities should function today. It is a earthly model of the spiritual state of Anand. A place of endless love and joy, where all are welcome. When a Sikh takes Amrit, no matter where in the world they were born, they always belong to Anandpur Sahib. Anandpur Sahib is always the home of a Sikh. A Sikh is never homeless. Anandpur Sahib is the home of the Khalsa, it is always our palace, we are one family, all born in the city of Anand. There are no words to describe the significance of Anandpur Sahib in the heart of a Khalsa.

A Thorn in the Eye of Cruelty.

Guru Gobind Singh Ji created the Khalsa army to be a thorn in the eye of cruelty. A Khalsa should be a bully's worst nightmare. The Khalsa should always stand up for those who have no voice. Those who were hopeless, those who had been stomped on, those who society had caste out, the Khalsa welcomed and protected them. The Khalsa gave them courage and honor. Guru Gobind Singh Ji and the Khalsa willingly left their comfortable lives to take on the fight of the poor and oppressed. There are many incidents when young women were kidnapped and their own parents did not want to protect them, because they were afraid of the government's wrath. The Khalsa would then rescue these women from the government palaces. When they brought the women home, their parents would not accept them. The women then also joined the Khalsa as soldiers. The Khalsa uplifted those who society deemed worthless and showed them how to find their inner strength and divinity. It was said that the Khalsa is a thorn in the eye of cruelty that is stuck so deep, that the body can die, the eye can decompose, but the thorn will never leave the eye. This means that a true Khalsa will never cease to protect those who are being mistreated and made to feel inferior.

The Khalsa continued to reside at Anandpur Sahib and never ceased to fight for humanity. The Sikhs became stronger and stronger. Around Anandpur Sahib, there were kingdoms in the hills which were ruled by the hill chiefs (pahari rajay). These hill chiefs often clashed with the Guru and felt threatened by his power and appeal. One day a large group of the chiefs came to Guru Gobind Singh Ji, and said that they wanted to take Amrit, the Sikh baptism, and become a part of the Khalsa army.

The hill chiefs said they would take Amrit under one condition. They wanted to be baptized separately from the Sikhs whose background was that of lower castes. One of the important aspects of the Sikh Baptism is that anyone who wants to be baptized drinks the Amrit from the same vessel. This symbolizes equality and equal membership in the Gurus army. Men, women, young, old, rich, poor, high caste, king, low caste, anyone from any faith, all were equal, and all drank from the same vessel. They all took the same vows and became one family. This eliminated all distinctions and made everyone equal. However, this did not fit well with those who wanted to keep others beneath them. Many felt anger and jealousy when they saw those who came from low castes wear the Sikh turban and dared to walk with pride. In those days, pride only belonged to the rich and high caste. The turban was worn by royals and nobles. Many high caste egos could not endure the fact that those whose necks they kept under their feet, they now took "Amrit" and dared to walk as equals with their heads held high. Some Sikhs, who belonged to low caste background before joining the Khalsa, were even physically attacked, on the way to visiting Anandpur Sahib.

Guru Gobind Singh Ji refused to let the hill chiefs drink from a separate vessel. He stood up for the low castes and refused to allow the hill chiefs to disrespect them. This made the hill chiefs even more angry. This incident was the start of the battles which would eventually lead to the shahadat of Guru Gobind Singh Jis sahibzaday. If Guru Gobind Singh Ji would have allowed the hill chiefs to drink from a separate vessel, millions of people would have become Sikh. Each hill chief would have taken Amrit and become Sikh along with his Kingdom. However, Guru Gobind Singh Ji never cared about his number of followers or quantity of Sikhs. Guru Ji only cared about quality and principle. Guru Gobind Singh Ji refused to let the hill chiefs put divisions in the Khalsa.

The conflict between the hill chiefs and the Khalsa escalated greatly. Even though the Khalsa was outrageously outnumbered, each Sikh fought with fearlessness and with great spirit. After many defeats, the hill chiefs joined forces with King Aurangzeb. Over a million troops were sent to surround the Anandpur Sahib Fortress. Aurangzeb had bragged that Sikhs were so outnumbered that each soldier could pick up a handful of dirt, throw it on the city, and the whole city of Anandpur Sahib would be burried alive in hours. However, after 8 months of a long and hard battle, the Sikhs were giving enemy forces a run for their money.

Things were difficult for the Sikhs too. Food and supplies ran short. The Sikhs were hungry and sleep deprived. Sikhs would risk their lives to bring food back to the fort. They had made a small hole in the wall of the fort and Sikhs would leave to get supplies and come back. Here, we must pause to think about the spirit of the Sikhs. They were living in these conditions willingly. They could have left anytime; they could have gone out of the hole in the wall and not come back to battle. They could have escaped when getting food. However, their love and devotion were so strong that they braved these harsh circumstances willingly, over and over. They always came back. One day the Sikhs that left to get food were killed. The enemy forces had found out about the hole. After that, it was difficult for Sikhs to obtain food and supplies and they faced starvation. We must never forget the bravery of our Sikh ancestors and what they faced to give us Sikhi.

Leaving Anandpur Sahib out of Respect for Hinduism and Islam

Six months passed like this. Despite the harsh conditions, Sikhs were still ready to defend Anandpur Sahib and fight Aurangzeb's cruelty till their last beath. On the 6th of the Month of Poh, in 1704, the enemy troops came to the Sikhs with a request. They asked the Sikhs to leave the fortress of Anandpur Sahib. They promised that the Sikhs would be granted safe passage, however Guru Gobind Singh Ji knew this was a lie.

The enemy forces urged Guru Gobind Singh Ji to grant their request and leave Anandpur Sahib. They swore on everything they held holy that the Sikhs would not be attacked if they left the fort. Guru Gobind Singh Ji refused their request each time, knowing their plan. After many attempts, the enemy forces wrote oaths on the pages of the holy Quaran, promising that if the Sikhs were to leave, they would not be attacked. The Hindu hill chiefs also sent over

Priest Pamma with small sculptures of cows.[39] The troops requested Guru Gobind Singh Ji to believe them, in the name of the holy cow and holy Quaran.

As a child, Guru Gobind Singh Ji sacrificed his father for religious freedom. Now too, Guru Gobind Singh Ji showed utmost reverence for other faiths. Guru Ji taught that it is important to empathize, to feel the emotions of others. We live in a world where people play with the feelings of those who are kind and abuse the trust of the faithful. Even though the oaths were full of deceit, the messengers of the enemy forces came standing behind the pure religious sentiments of two faiths. The enemy forces were using these religious sentiments for a selfish purpose, but still Guru Ji accepted their request out of pure respect. Respecting all faiths is a principle that is crucial to the core of Sikhi.

When the enemy forces told Guru Ji to leave the fort for the sake of their perfidious oaths on the Quaran and Holy Cow, Guru Gobind Singh Ji had no choice but to show respect for the holy symbols by honoring the oaths. It turns out that Guru Gobind Singh Ji respected the symbols of these other religions, more than these troops who claimed to be followers. Even today, leaders use religion to commit atrocities and gain fame, however in their hearts they have no real love and respect for their religion. Religion is used as a toy, a way for politicians to play with a person's most sacred emotions. Here too, the enemy forces disrespected their own religion by swearing false oaths in the name of that which millions of followers held holy. Sikhs must be aware of those who take advantage of their faith for political gain.

Guru Gobind Singh Ji started preparing to leave Anandpur Sahib. Guru Ji gathered the Sikhs in a large

---

[39] The cow is considered sacred and protected in Hinduism.

formation and directed the Sikhs in the beginning of the formation to hold the "Nishan Sahib," the Khalsa flag. Guru Gobind Singh Ji knew that the enemy forces would not keep their promise, and that they would attack the Khalsa Army from behind. For this reason, Guru Gobind Singh Ji filled up many carts with bones, scraps, and other garbage. This way when the enemy troops attacked, they would not get supplies. Before leaving, Guru Gobind Singh Ji burned the Sikh canons and weapons so that they would not land in enemy hands. Guru Gobind Singh Ji took all the books with him as well. Guru Gobind Singh Ji also kept his best warriors at the end of the formation. Guru Gobind Singh Ji knew that the enemy forces would follow and attack. Since the enemy attack would come from behind, Guru Gobind Singh Ji maintained the best warriors towards the back end of the formation. This way, when the enemy forces attacked the Sikhs, the Sikhs would be prepared. Guru Gobind Singh Ji writes about this incident in *Zafarnama*.[40]

Guru Gobind Singh Ji requested one Sikh to stay back. Bhai Gurbaksh Ji volunteered even though this meant definite shahadat. As the Sikhs left, Bhai Gurbaksh Ji felt pain in being separated from his beloved Guru and Sikh family. Guru Gobind Singh Ji told Bhai Gurbaksh Ji that separation of bodies is not true separation, as long as the heart is connected. Gurbani says "The union of the heart is the only true union, that alone can be called togetherness."[41] Guru Gobind Singh Ji embraced Bhai Gurbaksh Ji and told him that when he reads Gurbani, and looks within himself, when he sees his reflection, in all those moments, he would be able to see Guru Gobind Singh Ji with him.

---

[40] Letter to Aurangzeb written by Guru Gobind Singh Ji after the Shahadat of Sahibzaday
[41] Guru Granth Sahib Jee, 724

After visiting Gurudwara Sis Ganj Sahib, where the head of Guru Gobind Singh Ji's blessed father, Guru Teg Bahadur Ji was cremated, the Sikhs left the city of bliss. Anandpur Sahib was such a special place where each corner was full of the love of Guru Gobind Singh Ji. The town that was barren but become lush when the Guru placed his feet there. An example for the world, unmatched today, a place free from hunger, hatred, greed, and ego. A place where there was no stranger, and no worries. A place where all lived in the presence of God. Imagine for a moment the difficulty and heartache, that the Sikhs felt upon leaving. Today, with heavy hearts the Sikhs left this place, once again left their comforts, to comfort the down-trodden and oppressed children of God. Such selfless love is rare in this world's darkness. It is incumbent upon Sikhs to remember how our ancestors paved the road of Sikhi and sacrificed everything in love for humanity, and how lucky we are to be part of this tradition where selfless love and seva know no boundaries.

PART ONE: THE NIGHT OF 7 POH AT GURUDWARA CHHANN BABA KUMA MASKHI JI

Prayer is More Precious than Life.

After the Sikhs left Anandpur Sahib, they spent the night walking towards the Sirsa River. The night passed and it was Amrit Vela.[42] It is here that Guru Gobind Singh Ji told the Sikhs to sit and pray. This was a very important lesson. No matter how hectic life gets, God should be the center of everything. Just as air is important for our body, prayer is important for our spirit. The Sikhs are always thirsty for prayer, always longing for the chance to praise God. For this reason, even though tens of thousands of enemy forces were approaching, the Sikhs sat down for prayer. Guru Gobind Singh Ji performed "Jap Ji Sahib" and "Asa-di-Vaar," which is the "nitnem," or daily prayer for sangat.[43]

When someone's trying to escape a dangerous situation, they normally do not pause or go back. For example, imagine someone's house is on fire. A person would try to get out as fast as they can. They would not stay in their house, nor would they run back in, unless there is something inside which is more important than their lives. For example, A parent may run inside a burning house to save the life of their child. A spouse might risk his or her life for their partner. However, no one puts their life in peril, unless it is for something incredibly precious to them, more precious than their own life.

For these Sikhs, their prayers and relationship to the divine was more precious than their own lives. This relationship gave their spirits life. The same Sikhs went who

---

[42] The time that Sikhs pray, usually used to refer to early morning hours.
[43] Jap Ji Sahib is the daily morning prayer for Sikhs, part of the five daily banis (prayers) which are read by Sikhs individually. Asa-di-Vaar is the daily morning prayer for Sikhs which Sikhs often read together in Sangat.

bodies went hungry for months, they did not let their soul go hungry for even a day. This shows us that the body is made for the comfort of the soul. Our body is like the jewelry box, and our soul is the diamond inside. We can sacrifice the comfort of the body for the life of the spirit, because the spirit is who we are, it is our reality. To sacrifice the health of our soul for bodily comforts is a foolish and losing bargain. For a Sikh, we care for and respect our body, because it is the home for our soul. However, if there is no soul, then the body is dust. That is why Sikhs allowed their bodies to feel danger but did not let their souls starve. Many people in this world will let their souls and conscience die for the sake of their body. For a Sikh, the comforts of the body body will always come after the needs of the soul

Guru Gobind Singh Ji taught how precious Nitnem (daily routine prayers) is for a Sikh. It is more precious than life. Guru Gobind Singh Ji put his life at stake, and even the lives of his children, family, and beloved Sikhs, in order to stop and pray. Even in a warzone, one must not become disconnected from their prayers. After all, it was these prayers that were giving the Sikhs the strength to fight such a difficult battle. It was these prayers that made Sikhs saint-soldiers, and not merely soldiers. When times are dark, frantic, and scary, and it is hardest to pray, that is when we need prayer the most.

This incident shows that not only is it important to pray even more during difficult times, but it is important to be grateful. According to Allah Yaar Khan Jogi Ji, Guru Gobind Singh Ji and the Sikhs did "Shahbaz". The word "Shahbaz" means "thanks." The Sikhs sat down and lovingly spent time in gratitude, thanking God. Even when a Sikh is in pain or loss, they should recognize that this pain is also God's loving gift. Pain is a teacher for our soul. Without pain there is no passion or compassion. The greater the pain, the

50

more important it is to take time out and thank God for his blessings. During this time of despair, the Sikhs took time to be grateful. Gratitude is always important; however, it is most important for the spirit during hard times.

A Promise Broken

Even in the middle of danger, the Sikh's hearts were not afraid. They continued to sing to God lovingly and lost themselves in the blissful beauty of God's praise. As expected, the enemy forces started to attack. They engaged in perfidy, one of the most treacherous of war crimes till today. They did not care that the Sikhs were deep in prayer. Allah Yaar Khan Jogi Ji expressed his pain at their attack in his poetry. For Muslims, it is taboo to disturb someone who is praying let alone attack them. Religious Muslims do not even walk past a person, or in front of a person, who is praying. Here, those claiming to fight in the name of Islam were breaking the rules of Islam left and right. It goes to show that false people have no religion. They are Godless. They may claim to be Muslim, or Hindu, or Sikh, but a true Muslim, Sikh, or Hindu is never cruel to anyone.

After Amrit Vela, Guru Gobind Singh Ji told the Sikhs that it is time to cross the Sirsa River. At the back of the Sikh formation were the best fighters, including Baba Ajit Singh Ji, the oldest biological son of Guru Gobind Singh Ji. They fought and kept the enemy forces engaged as the Sikhs in the front of the line crossed over.

It is here that the Sikhs were separated. The river was swollen and there was a treacherous current. Mother Gujri and the younger Sahibzaday, Baba Zorawar Singh Ji (age 9), and Baba Fateh Singh Ji (age 7) ended up together. Guru Gobind Singh Ji, the older sahibzaday Baba Ajit Singh Ji (age 17) and Baba Jujhar Singh Ji (age 13), as well as about

51

40 Sikhs ended up separate from Mother Gujri Ji. Out of 400, only 40 Sikhs were left with Guru Gobind Singh Ji after the river crossing. Some had obtained shahadat fighting and others had been engulfed by the waves of the Sirsa. Bhai Jevan Singh Jee[44], the Sikh who had brought back the head of Guru Teg Bahadur Ji to Guru Gobind Singh Ji, was one of the Gursikhs who had obtained shahadat prior to reaching the Sirsa River. Mother Sundri Ji Bhai Dhana Singh Ji, Bhai Jawahar Singh Ji, Bhai Mani Singh Ji, (son-in law of Bhai Lakhi Shah Vanjara Ji and the husband of Bibi Seeto Ji), some sevadaars including Bibi Beebo and Bibi Bhago, and Mother Sahib Kaur Ji were also separated from both groups. They walked towards Delhi, to stay with Bhai Lakhi Shah Vanjara Ji[45].

---

[44] Upon taking Amrit, Bhai Jaita Ji's changed his name to Bhai Jeewan Singh Ji.

[45] As a reminder, Bhai Lakhi Shah Vanjara Ji was the Sikh who cremated the body of Guru Teg Bahadur Ji in his own house. He was the father-in-law of Bhai Mani Singh Ji. Bhai Mani Singh Ji was married to Bhai Lakhi Shah Vanjara Ji's daughter, Bibi Seeto Ji. Bhai Mani Singh Ji later became the head priest of Harmandir Sahib. Bhai Mani Singh Ji also became shaheed, when he gave his life by warning Sikhs, to protect them from a government ambush that was to take place during a Sikh gathering at Harmandir Sahib. Bhai Mani Singh was executed by the government at age 94. He was cut limb by limb. This is symbolic, because the sword injuries that would have been inflicted on the bodies of the whole Sikh community, were inflicted on his body alone. Bhai Mani Singh Ji took the pain of the community on his own body. That is the ideal for how a Sikh leader should be. Bhai Lakhi Shah Vanjara Ji not only came from a family of great gursikh warriors and shaheeds, but his descendants were also well-known warriors and shaheeds.

The Love of Baba Kuma Maskhi Ji.

Mother Gujri Ji and the younger sahibzaday spent the night at the house of Baba Kuma Maski Ji.[46] Baba Kuma Maski Ji was a Muslim Devotee of Guru Gobind Singh Ji. It is here that the first smagam of Safar-e-Shahadat is held. Baba Kuma Maski Jee helped people cross the river as a profession. He was poor financially but rich in generosity. He risked his life to keep Mother Gujri Ji and the sahibzaday in his small hut. This was a death sentence at the time. Mother Gujri Ji, the sahibzaday, Guru Gobind Singh Ji, and all Sikhs were all highly wanted by authorities, who had tried endlessly to capture them.

On the first day of the smagam, Sikhs are blessed with the honor of sitting in the embrace of our Guru, in the blessed spot where the holy feet of Baba Zorawar Singh Ji, Baba Fateh Singh Ji, and Mother Gujri Ji once stood. It is here that Sikhs remember the love of Baba Kuma Mashki Ji. We remember the great favor he bestowed on our panth and how he took care of the precious wealth, the great assets of our panth, our dear sahibzaday.

Baba Kuma Maskhi Ji was born as a Muslim. He probably called upon God as Allah or Khuda. He must have read the kalma and prayed the Namaz. Although he was a Muslim, today every Sikh around the world breaks free from the boundaries of religious differences and keeps Baba Khuma Mashki Ji enshrined within the temple of their hearts. Sikhs are forever buried in gratitude for the favors that Baba Kuma Maskhi Ji has done for our panth. On one hand, people are able to buy others with money. Many will sell out for a price. People will even sell their morals. Yet, Baba Kuma

---

[46] Baba Kuma Maski Ji's real name was Karim Baksh, but he is popularly called Kuma Maski due to his occupation.

Mashki Ji has won over and bought our whole kaum[47], not with money, but with his warm kindness. With his blessed efforts and selfless service, he has purchased us all. He has won all our hearts.

Men who claimed to belong to the religion of Baba Kuma Maskhi Ji, had tried countless times to make the Sikh Kaum bow down in fear. Their sword was unable to make a single member of our kaum bow. Yet, the love of Kuma Mashki, is powerful enough to make our whole kaum bow down before him in respect and gratitude. Today we sit here with our heads bowed in reverence and appreciation of his pure and godly love. His goodness weighs upon us so greatly that we have no choice but to bow in appreciation.

Baba Zorawar Singh Ji and Baba Fateh Singh Ji have paved the way. They have shown us the path that Sikhs must follow. Baba Kumba Mashki Ji has also followed this path and thus we lovingly venerate him. That is why it is crucial to say a few words today, in order to remember this pure soul and honor him with our heartfelt respect, adoration, and reverence.

It is in this hut that the younger sahibzaday and Mother Gujri spent the night. A neighbor named Bibi Lakshmi Jee bought food for them. Baba Kuma Maskhi Jee was physically poor and may not have had enough food to eat himself. He had very few possessions, lived in a small hut, and had only a broken bed that he put Mother Gujri and the younger Sahibzaday on. As they slept, Baba Kuma Maskhi Ji stood in reverence with folded hands and kept guard. He gave everything he had to Mother Ji and the Sahibzaday, even his warm clothes. He protected and cared for the elderly mother and the angelic young children of

---

[47] The word "kaum" refers to the Sikh nation.

Guru Gobind Singh Ji. For this reason, we are blessed to sit in this very spot and give thanks to poor man's rich heart.

As Mother Gujri Ji hugged the younger sahibzaday and patted their heads until they fell asleep, Baba Zorawar Singh Ji and Baba Fateh Singh Ji asked where all the other Sikhs were. They asked where all their brothers were. All the Sikhs had lived like a family at Anandpur Sahib. Now they were in a hut in a jungle, and their loved ones were nowhere to be seen. Baba Zorawar Singh Ji and Baba Fateh Singh Ji had never been separated from their brothers, and their Anandpur Sahib sangat family. They were used to the love and joy of Anandpur Sahib.

Allah Yaar Khan Jogi Ji describes a beautiful conversation[48] that the younger sahibzaday have with their blessed grandmother. Baba Jorawar Singh Ji and Baba Fateh Singh Ji ask *"Where are our brothers, our companions, and the soldiers? Our brothers have forgotten all about us in their passion for the struggle. They have become so engulfed that they lost themselves, how can they even remember us."* In their sweet innocent voices, they tell Mother Gujri that, *"now when we see our brothers and sangat family, when we see our father, we will be angry. Our brothers, our mother, and our father, will all take turns. They will keep hugging us and saying loving words to try to pacify our anger. They will keep saying don't be angry. But we will stay angry. They will request us over and over to forgive them. We won't budge. Then we will make them promise never to leave us again. Only then will be forgive them."* Mother Gujri then lovingly replied, *"Now when you meet your brothers, you will meet them in a way that you will never again be separate."*

---

[48] Shaheedan-E-Wafa, stanzas 48-50

Mother Gujri was very close to God and could feel what was coming.

Today we are blessed to sit in the hut of Baba Kuma Maskhi Ji. What was once a small hut is now a huge gurudwara. Baba Kuma Maskhi Ji once did not have enough money to feed Mother Gujri Ji and the Sahibzaday. Now all of Mother Gujri's precious grandchildren, are here eating langar at this Gurudwara. Here, the hungry are fed, given shelter, and love. That is the power of compassion. The good deed and love of Baba Kuma Maskhi Ji has grown infinitely and today thoushands sit and remember him. We sit at the spot where Mother Gujri Ji and the Sahibzaday did *rehiras sahib*[49], they prayed, and meditated on Waheguru. We sit at the spot where a saint sacrificed his life to serve his guru, a place of great power and godly energy.

A Promise Kept by a Virtuous Daughter

While Mother Gujri and the younger Sahibzaday were at the hut of Baba Kuma Maskhi Jee, Guru Gobind Singh Ji, the older Sahibzaday, and 40 Sikhs headed towards Chamkaur Sahib. It is here that Guru Gobind Singh Ji visited Bhai Nihung Khan Pathan Ji. Bhai Nihung Khan Pathan Ji was a Muslim devotee of Guru Gobind Singh Ji. Their love was so strong that Bhai Nihung Khan Pathan Ji had dedicated his life to the Khalsa's cause. Bhai Nihung Khan Pathans Ji's father, Bhai Nurang Khan Ji, was a devotee of Guru Hargobind Sahib Ji. Guru Ji had visited their house many times. Today Bhai Nihung Khan Pathan Ji invited Guru Gobind Singh Ji and the Sikhs to their house despite the danger that they could face. Enemy soldiers were going door to door looking for Guru Ji and the Sikhs. They were killing anyone who offered food or shelter to the Sikh army.

---

[49] Sikh evening prayer

Bhai Nihung Khan Pathan Ji was connected to God and was not afraid of any man; let alone any cruel tyrant. He risked his life to have Guru Gobind Singh Ji come over.

Two of the Gursikhs who accompanied Guru Gobind Singh Ji were very injured. One was Bhai Bachittar Singh Ji[50], the son of Bhai Mani Singh Ji and the maternal grandson of Bhai Lakhi Shah Vanjara Ji. The other was Baba Zorawar Singh Ji Bassi Pathana Vale. Baba Zorawar Singh was lovingly known as the fifth son of Guru Gobind Singh Ji. While all the Sikhs were considered children of Guru Gobind Singh Ji, Baba Zorawar Singh Ji lived with Guru Ji since he was a very young child. Baba Zorawar Singh Ji had the same name as Sahibzada Baba Zorawar Singh Ji and was around the same age as Baba Jujhar Singh Ji, a young teenager at this time. Guru Gobind Singh Ji loved him a lot and he was lovingly known as the fifth Sahibzada. Baba Zorawar Singh Ji was from the village of Bassi Pathana, near the city of Sirhind. His parents were named Bhai Nathu Ram Lota Ji and Mother Subhiki Ji. After Baba Zorawar Singh Ji's parents died, Guru Gobind Singh Ji lovingly raised him alongside the Sahibzaday.

Guru Gobind Singh Ji told two Sikhs, Bhai Bagga Singh Ji, and Bhai Gursa Singh Ji, to take Baba Zorawar Singh Ji to his paternal aunt's (bhua ji's) house, so that he could get medical aid and rest. They took him in a cart (gadda). Baba Zorawar Singh Ji's injuries were not as bad as Bhai Bachittar Singh Ji's and he was able to travel. Baba Zorawar Singh Ji went to his aunt's house in the village of Dadheri, where his

---

[50] Bhai Bachitar Singh Ji was a great warrior, who is well known for his bravery and for fighting in one-on-one combat against a drunk elephant that was sent by enemy forces at Fort Lohgarh. Enemy forces tried to break through the fort, by covering an intoxicated elephant in armor and putting a large blade in the elephant's trunk. Bhai Bachitar Singh Ji caused the elephant to reverse direction and attack the enemy forces.

aunt Bibi Pupan Ji cared for his injuries. If Guru Gobind Singh Ji or any of the Sikhs wanted, they could have also left. Guru Gobind Singh Ji could have protected Baba Ajit Singh Ji and Baba Jujhar Singh Ji by also sending them with Baba Zorawar Singh Ji. However, Guru Ji and the Sikhs refused to give up. It was their faith in God and their dedication to humanity which stopped them from giving up even when things looked hopeless.

Bhai Bachitar Singh Ji had severe injuries and it did not seem like his body would survive. Guru Gobind Singh Ji left Bhai Bachittar Singh Ji in the care of Bhai Nihung Khan Pathan Ji and headed towards the small fort ("haveli") known as Chamkaur Sahib. Guru Gobind Singh Ji left fast because he did not want soldiers to find the Sikhs and start a battle at the house of Bhai Nihung Khan Pathan Ji, which also had a fort. Even though Bhai Nihung Khan Pathan knew that this was a risk, he still wanted Guru Ji to visit.

Allah Yaar Khan Jogi Ji writes that upon seeing the small fort, Guru Gobind Singh Ji said, *"The place that we are destined to come, it is here. The place where my children are to be cut piece by piece, this is that blessed place."* Jogi Ji also says that in all of India, Chamkaur Sahib is the only true place worthy of pilgrimage, the only true shrine, where a father sacrificed his children for dharma. This haveli was visited by Guru Nanak Dev Ji and had a deep beautiful history with the Gurus. Guru Gobind Singh Ji came to this blessed place once more.

During this time, enemy soldiers were going house to house looking for Guru Gobind Singh Ji and the Sikhs. They soon came to the house of Bhai Nihung Khan Pathan Ji. Bhai Bachittar Singh Ji knew his time to leave his body was coming soon, so he sat and lovingly meditated on God. Bhai Nihung Khan Pathan Ji told his daughter, Bibi Mumtaz Ji, to sit with Bhai Bachittar Singh, and make sure no one disturbed his prayers. They both sat in the room of Bibi Mumtaz Ji. When the soldiers came, they searched his whole house except for the room that Bibi Mumtaz Ji and Bhai Bachittar Singh Ji were in. This was because Bhai Nihung Khan Pathan Ji told the soldiers that his daughter and son in law were resting in that room and that they should not go in there.

The soldiers eventually left without searching that room. However, Bibi Mumtaz Ji heard the words of her father. Out of deep respect for her saintly father, Bibi Mumtaz Ji said that she will honor his word. Bibi Ji said, "since you called him your son in law with your holy and blessed mouth, I will consider him my husband forever." During those days, a person of honor was known for how they kept their word. If an honorable person made a promise, or gave their word, they kept it at all costs. Bhai Bachitar Singh Ji had obtained shahadat during the time he was in the room with Bibi Mumtaz Ji. Still Bibi Mumtaz Ji said she wanted to consider him her husband. Bibi Ji never married, even though she lived to 125 years of age. This was an act of deep love and respect for her father. Bibi Mumtaz Ji loved her father so much, and in a culture where your word is everything, Bibi Ji never wanted her saintly father's word to be proven false. On one side you have those soldiers whose word had no value, and here you have a daughter making such a great sacrifice to honor her father's word. Bibi Mumtaz Ji, the saintly daughter of Nihung Khan Pathan Ji, was the embodiment of love, respect, and good character.

A Love Unmatched

Guru Gobind Singh Ji reached the haveli of Chamkaur Sahib that night. After many days the Gursikhs were able to rest. It takes great faith to fall asleep when there is danger lurking above your heads. These Sikhs trusted God, so they slept with ease. Since there were no beds, the Sikhs slept on the rugs they had under the saddles of their horses. They put those rugs on the floor and slept on them. The Sikhs all fell into deep sleep. They were not afraid or nervous about the danger surrounding them. Gurbani says *"I sleep worry free, and I do not worry when awake, because I know God is working within everyone, everywhere, and in everything."*[51]

Guru Gobind Singh Ji sat awake for a while with his head bowed down and chanted *"Waheguru Waheguru Waheguru, Tuhi Tu Tuhi Tu* (Wonderful Guru, you alone you)." Guru Ji prayed "Dear God, I am happy in your will. Please may I only leave Chamkaur Sahib after becoming *"sukhroo."*[52] Most parents would think that Guru Gobind Singh Ji would pray for his life or the life of his children. However, as a parent, Guru Gobind Singh Ji prayed that all his children would fight bravely, not fear death, and give their lives for the struggle of Dharma. This is the difference between a parent of faith and a parent of the world.

This prayer was the prayer of many Gursikh parents. In 1773, when Shaheed Bhai Subegh Singh Ji was captured by the government, alongside his teenage son Bhai Shabaaz Singh Ji, both father and son were given a chance to leave their faith and have their lives spared. When they both

---

[51] Guru Granth Sahib Ji, 1136
[52] "Sukhroo" means successful after performing a duty. Guru Ji is saying may I leave after fully fulfilling my duty (sacrificing everything for dharma).

refused, the government sentenced them to be executed by being crushed to death between two rotating wheels which had blades sticking out (called a charkharhi). When Bhai Subegh Singh Ji was asked his last wish, he asked if his son Bhai Shabaaz Singh Ji could be executed first. The government asked why. Bhai Subegh Singh Ji said it will make his soul happy and proud, to see his son's bravery in the face of death. It would give him peace to know that he fulfilled his duty as a father, and he could die knowing that his son lived and died with his principles intact. It is the duty of every Sikh parent to raise children who fearlessly fight to make this world more just.

As night fell, some Sikhs slept, and some kept guard in case of an attack. Guru Gobind Singh Ji then told all the Sikhs to sleep and that today he would keep guard. Guru Gobind Singh Ji wanted to serve his beloved Sikhs. He knew that they would attain Shahadat the next day. Guru Ji looked at his family, the precious gursikhs, knowing that tomorrow most of their bodies would be gone. Guru Ji looked at Baba Ajit Singh Ji and Baba Jujhar Singh Ji one last time. Guru Ji went around hugged each Sikh and kissed their foreheads and necks.

Guru Gobind Singh Ji walked around the Gursikhs and lovingly watched them as they slept. Allah yaar Khan Jogi Ji describes Guru Ji watching the Gursikhs sleep like a parent lovingly watches their child sleep. The bodies of the Sikhs were tired and worn out with hunger. Guru Gobind Singh Ji knew the next day that these Gursikhs would obtain shahadat. Guru Gobind Singh Ji looked at the face of each Gursikh, one at a time. Tomorrow these faces that Guru Ji loved would be gone. Guru Ji looked at each Sikh with love, including Baba Ajit Singh Ji and Baba Jujhar Singh Ji. Tomorrow the Sikhs would fight, their bodies would be shaheed in battle, and their souls would become immortal.

61

Guru Ji walked around the gursikhs tightly hugging each one of them, clasping them against his heart. Guru Ji knew this was the last time he would hug his children and dear gursikhs, all as beloved as his sons, before they all attained martyrdom.

As Guru Ji looked at each Sikh, his eyes were filled with oceans of love. Guru Gobind Singh Ji himself was the embodiment of love. It was his love for humanity which brought him here. Guru Ji could not take another step past the Sikhs. Guru ji froze, his heart full of love for his Sikh family. The love between Guru Ji and the Sikhs was a connection greater than any other. Guru Gobind Singh Ji walked by his Sikhs and fixed their turbans, which were coming off. Guru Gobind Singh Ji cleaned the dirt off their faces with his own clothes. Some of the Sikhs were sleeping with their heads at a weird angle (they were using saddles as pillows). Guru Gobind Singh Ji fixed their heads so they would not hurt at night, even though tomorrow the necks and heads of these soldiers would feel unbearable pain as they were severed in battle.

Guru Gobind Singh Ji then started massaging each Sikh. The bodies of the Sikhs were sore from months of combat. Guru Ji lovingly took care of their soreness and injuries. As Guru Ji massaged each Sikh, he started kissing their foreheads and necks, the necks that would be cut with swords tomorrow. Guru Gobind Singh Ji then massaged the bodies, the legs, and feet of the Sikhs. While massaging the feet of each gursikh, Guru Gobind Singh Ji started kissing each one of their feet repeatedly. Such infinite love of a Guru for his disciples had never been seen before! Such humble love! Such deep love! A Guru kissing the feet of disciples was unheard of! Allah Yaar Khan Jogi Ji describes this scene and this love by concluding, *"I swear over God and Guru*

Nanak Dev Ji, no matter how much we praise Guru Gobind Singh Ji it is not enough."

PART TWO: THE NIGHT OF 8 POH AT GURUDWARA ATTACK SAHIB

Kehri Becomes Saheri

There once was a village named Kheri. The word "kheri" means blossoming in happiness. Today, the village is called Saheri. The word "saheri" means to bear a burden. This refers to the burden of a grave sin. A sin committed by a man who once worked in the house of the Guru. A man who the guru had helped and taken care of. A man who betrayed Mother Gujri Ji's trust and acted heartlessly, due to his greed. A man who until this day is known as Gangu Paapi (Gangu the sinner).

Gangu invited Mother Gujri Ji and the sahibzaday to his house. He pretended to care about them. At one point they had spent time together, when Gangu spent time working as a cook in the house of Guru Gobind Singh Ji. They had treated him like a member of the family. On this 8th night of Poh, Gangu invited Mother Gujri and the younger Sahibzaday to stay at his house.

However, Gangu's intentions were evil. His mind was filled with greed. Outside he acted pure and kind. He assured Mother Gujri that all would be okay. Gangu had more money than Baba Kuma Maskhi Ji. He was able to give Mother Gujri Ji a bed, better food, and a bigger room to sleep in. Gangu had money, but he was incredibly poor. So poor, that he did not have any mercy in his evil heart for the innocent children and elderly mother of Guru Gobind Singh Ji. In Sikhi, knowledge is not enough to be a good Sikh. Gangu spent years in the Gurudwara, and in the sangat, yet his heart had not been softened. Gangu not only heard the teachings of Gurbani, but he also likely heard Gurbani so many times that he had a good amount memorized. However, knowledge without emotions and actions is worthless. Look around today, you will see many people who have knowledge. You will see people who have

Gurbani memorized yet their actions are the complete opposite of what the Guru taught.

One time, Sikhs asked Guru Gobind Singh Ji how people can be surrounded constantly by Gurbani and sangat, yet they do not mend their ways. Guru Gobind Singh Ji then filled three buckets of water. In one bucket, Guru Gobind Singh Ji placed rocks, In the second bucket Guru Ji placed dirt. In the third bucket, Guru Gobind Singh Ji placed sugar candies (patasas). Guru Gobind Singh Ji, then said the water represents sangat. In all three buckets the water is the same. In the same way, the sangat is the same for everyone. However, the rocks, dirt, and sugar candies represent the types of people who come to sangat. The first type are akin to rocks. They look like they are immersed in sangat from the outside, but inside they are still hardened. In this way, many people outwardly look like they are immersed in sangat. They may spend a lot of time in sangat, yet the message of sangat does not touch them and does not change them. Today, you will see many people who do read Gurbani and follow outward aspects of Sikhi. However, their hearts are still full of anger and hatred. These types of people are like the rocks.

Then there are some people who are like the dirt. They come into sangat with bad thoughts in their minds. Not only do they not change, but they negatively impact those around them, just as the dirt makes the water muddy. The third type of people are like the sugar candies. The sugar candies come into the water hardened, but they soon change. They melt and dissolve in the water. This makes the water sweet. In the same way, some people come to sangat and allow the message to touch their hearts. They lose themselves and lose their egos. They themselves are sweet and they sweeten the lives of those around them with their kindness. They are receptive to change. This is the right way to do sangat. One must be willing to accept the teachings in one's own life.

Those who follow the teachings of Gurbani become angels. They become God like. To become a Sikh is leave your negative qualities behind and adopt the qualities of God as described in Gurbani. Just sitting in sangat is not enough. Listening with the ears is not enough. One must have an open and receptive heart. Knowledge alone is not enough, if a person still has greed and ego within them. Guru Granth Sahib Ji says, "A person makes many efforts but still their souls are not softened, how did they reach God's court this way?"[53] A person cannot reach God with a stiff heart. In tav parsad savaiye[54], Guru Gobind Singh Ji tells us that people can read all the scriptures of the earth and sky, but still if there is no love, it is all useless.[55] Gangu may have had sangat and knowledge, but he was lacking love and emotion. That is why he fell prey to greed.

Out of his greed, Gangu turned Mother Gujri and the younger sahibzaday in to the authorities. This would lead to a huge reward from the government. Gangu would become rich at the cost of these innocent lives. Gangu let the whole village know that Mother Gujri and the sahibzaday were at his house. Gangu yelled and called over all the villagers. They held Mother Gujri Ji and the sahibzaday, while the local leaders and officers arrived to arrest them. Gangu was not just a person, but Gangu is also a mindset. Today, there are many gangus who hurt our children, and our innocent citizens, due to their greed. There are Gangu's disguised as Sikhs. They may have a lot of knowledge about religion but they do not have love. They dirty their souls for the sake of

---

[53] Guru Granth Sahib Ji, 278
[54] One of the Sikh morning prayers
[55] Dasam Bani, 12

67

wealth. They have no loyalty and will even stab those who have done good to them. These gangus are everywhere, and their selfishness is the reason for their misery and the misery of this world.

The Battle of Chamkaur Sahib Begins

As the younger sahibzaday and Mother Gujri spent the night of 8 Poh at the house of Gangu, Guru Gobind Singh Ji, the elder Sahibzaday, and beloved gursikhs spent the day fighting the battle of Chamkaur Sahib. Aurangzeb sent over a million troops in pursuit of Guru Gobind Singh Ji and the Sikhs. They surrounded the haveli of Chamkaur. Guru Gobind Singh Ji describes this battle in *Zafarnama*, his letter to Aurangzeb.

As the enemy approached, the Sikhs left the fort in groups of five. This was part of the battle strategy of Guru Gobind Singh Ji. Sikhs would fight back-to-back, backs touching so that there was no space in the middle of them, and so that both sides were attacking the enemy and defending each other simultaneously. Each Sikh would defend the other Sikh from getting attacked from the back. This way of fighting required a deep trust between Sikhs.

Guru Gobind Singh Ji's ability as a general was incredible. It is mindboggling to fathom how the Sikhs were able to fight and win so many battles this outnumbered. Guru Gobind Singh Ji had the best weapons and strategy. The Sikhs knew how to use nature and their surroundings to fight even when greatly outnumbered. Guru Gobind Singh Ji made sure that the Sikhs had the best weapons available. These weapons often required great strength to use. This indicates the physical fitness of the Sikhs. Overall wellness, wellness of the mind, body, and spirit, were all important for Sikhs. In order to shoot the bow of Guru Gobind Singh Ji, a person had to have the strength to pull 225 kilograms of weight, with just the fingers that are used to pull back the arrow.

One time, Guru Gobind Singh Ji fought a one-on-one with General Painda Khan. General Painda Khan was considered the top archer in the nation. He had a desire to go one-on-one with Guru Gobind Singh Ji. Painda Khan would dream of killing Guru Gobind Singh Ji. It was his deepest wish to have a chance to shoot at him and face him in an archery match. It would be the top moment in his career. He would play the scene over and over in his mind.

The desire that was in a person's mind, that was the desire the Guru would fulfill. When Painda Khan came with an army to fight against the Khalsa, Guru Gobind Singh Ji, suggested that they engage in a one-on-one archery battle. Guru Gobind Singh Ji knew this was General Khan's desire The troops would stay behind and Guru Gobind Singh Ji and General Painda Khan would take turns shooting arrows. Painda Khan was famous for his archery and for never missing a target. He was sure he would kill Guru Gobind Singh Ji. General Painda Khan was covered in armor from head to toe. Guru Gobind Singh Ji did not have any armor on. Guru Gobind Singh Ji had a policy, he would never strike first. Guru Gobind Singh Ji gave General Painda Khan the first three chances to shoot. Painda Khan missed all three chances. This had never happened before.

Now, it was Guru Gobind Singh Ji's turn. Painda Khan lowered his helmet to cover his eyes and said, "I am covered head to toe in armor, where will you shoot?" The first and only arrow that Guru Gobind Singh Ji shot was able to poke through the hole in one of the metal rings of Painda Khan's chainmail, that was on the side of his helmet near his ear. This killed Painda Khan instantly, and all were shocked

69

at the precision of Guru Gobind Singh Jis arrow. Such precision comes from great faith and focus. Such focus comes from being connected to Waheguru.

Guru Gobind Singh Ji had a habit. He would give people a chance to fill their minds' desires. The same power is in Gurbani today. Many devotees of Gurbani will tell you that they see the thought and desires of their mind come alive before them. There is power in our mind's thoughts and there is power in perception. Many people who talk about spirituality will talk about the law of attraction. Guru Granth Sahib Ji also talks about this concept as being a law of God. Gurbani says *"Jio man dekhe par man taisa. Jaisee mansa taisee dasha."* This means, *"The way our mind is, that is how we perceive the minds of others. The way our thoughts, mindset, and desires are, that is how our reality and condition will be."* Our thoughts will manifest to become our destiny. That is why Gurbani teaches not only to control actions but to conquer our minds. Gurbani says *"Eh man jaisa seveh taisa hoyeh, tayhay karam kamaiye. Aapi beeji aapay hee khaavnaa kahnaa kicchu na jaaei."* Oh mind, you will become what you serve (focus on), your thoughts will determine the actions you take. According to your deeds, you will eat what you plant, there is nothing else to be said about this."[56] That is why positive thinking is so important. That is also why focusing on the virtues of the creator, and praising the creator, is incredibly important. When we praise God, we become God like. When we think great thoughts, we become great. Our environment greatly impacts our mindset. That is why it is important to seek the company of souls that you wish to become like. Company can change your thoughts instantly, thus changing the course of your destiny.

---

[56] Guru Granth Sahib Ji, 755

Take the example of Said Khan. Said Khan was a high-ranking officer in the Moghul army. He was taught and brainwashed to hate the Sikhs. One day, he was on a mission to kill Guru Gobind Singh Ji. This was the dream of many soldiers. For them, Guru Gobind Singh Ji was a prize to capture and kill. Part of the reason the Mughals captured the younger sahibzaday and elderly Mother Gujri, was that they were so frustrated that they had exhausted all their resources and still could not capture Guru Gobind Singh Ji.

On the way to try to capture Guru Gobind Singh Ji, Said Khan stayed at the house of his sister, Bibi Naseera. Bibi Naseera was a devout Sikh of Guru Gobind Singh Ji, she was also the wife of Pir Buddu Shah, one of Guru Gobind Singh Ji's devoted gursikhs. Bibi Naseera was delighted to see her brother after so long but was shocked to hear about his mission. Two of Bibi Naseera Ji's four sons gave their life fighting for human rights with the Sikh army. With pride, Bibi Naseera Ji said, "I regret that I could not sacrifice my remaining two sons for this noble cause." Such was the determination and struggle of Sikh mothers, who sacrificed everything for freedom and humanity.

Bibi Naseera Ji spent all night telling her brother how wonderful Guru Gobind Singh Ji is. She told him how he sacrificed so much for freedom and human dignity. Said Khan's heart melted. Naturally, he wanted to meet Guru Gobind Singh Ji, not to kill him anymore, but to see him. He desired to have a glimpse of such a great soul. Such was the power of Bibi Naseera's sangat. Even though it was just a few hours, the company of a blessed woman like Bibi Naseera was able to erase years of hatred that was in Said Khan's heart. Her company reformed her brother. Company changes your thoughts, which in turn, change your mindset and destiny. That is why the company of the holy is crucial for the soul.

Once more, we see the power of viewpoint of perception. For the downtrodden and oppressed, the Sikhs and the Guru were angels from God, who gave up their homes to fight for the meek. They served free food to all and stood up for human rights. That is the image Bibi Naseera showed Said Khan. However, the government put forth a different narrative. Defamation and propaganda are still used today, not only against Sikhs but against other groups as well. One must not blindly follow what they hear. It is important to be aware of false accusations and propaganda. Those in power will often put forth the most horrendous of accusations against their political opponents. Sikhs must be aware of such tactics. Some people called Guru Gobind Singh Ji an enemy, a rebel, and an infidel. Those like Allah Yaar Khan Jogi Ji called him the greatest of saints. Bhai Nand Lal Ji, a famous scholar who left his high ranking position as the personal tutor of Aurangzeb's son, and joined Guru Gobind Singh Ji, saw Guru Gobind Singh Ji as the image of the divine. When asked why he left his high paying job to live a harsh life among the Sikhs, Bhai Nand Lal Ji said, "In Aurangzeb's court, I may have had the fanciest of comforts, but even amid those comforts my spirit was slowly dying. Even in the hardships of Guru Gobind Singh Ji, my soul has found life." Just as a jeweler has the eye to look at a stone and determine its worth, it takes a spiritually trained eye to test the character of a person. For Sikhs, this eye is Guru Granth Sahib Ji. Before following the words of any human beings, Sikhs should use Gurbani as a thermometer or touchstone test. Otherwise, it is easy to be gullible and follow the wrong path. Our Guru's taught us to be vigilant and to worship with our eyes open. Let us pray to have the eyes of those like Bibi Naseera, Bhai Nand Lal Ji, and even Said Khan.

Not only was Guru Gobind Singh Ji a top-notch general but the way the Sikhs fought was unique and unparalleled. The way the Sikhs fought was more far more compassionate than even modern-day humanitarian law. In the law of armed conflict, there are rules for when it is justified to go to war (jus ad bellum) and rules for how to fight war justly (jus in bello). Today, the UN Charter has started to recognize humanitarian intervention as a just cause. Every single battle the Sikhs fought was for humanitarian intervention. When we look at modern day Geneva law, many skeptics say that it is impossible to enforce such rules on warfare. Others say that it is hard to win a war humanely. Not only did the Khalsa army only go to war for the noblest of causes, but they also held the highest humanitarian values and still were able to win. Astonishingly, the Khalsa army had the most incredible victories, always outnumbered. They are the only army to have ever successfully ruled over Afghanistan.

The Khalsa kept compassion at the core of everything. The Sikhs used arrows adorned with gold to shoot in the battlefield. That way if the enemy died, their family would not be left penniless. They could use the gold as currency. If the enemy was just injured, they would have gold to pay for their treatment. On the battlefield, the Sikhs would give water and first aid to enemy soldiers alongside their own. Bhai Khanaiya Ji, a loving Gursikh was given this mission from Guru Gobind Singh Ji. Bhai Khanaiya Ji told Guru Gobind Singh Ji that he does not see friend or enemy when he is in battle, he only sees God in everyone. Guru Gobind Singh Ji then blessed Bhai Khanaiya Ji and gave him bandages to use for first aid. This was over a century before the Red Cross was created.

Sikhs never attacked the women of the enemy, even though Sikh women were always attacked and kidnapped. Every enemy woman was accompanied back home with security from the Khalsa army. Sikhs never kept prisoners of war and never tortured the enemy. There are accounts of enemy spies being so impressed with the Sikh character that they gave up their missions and joined the Sikhs, even becoming martyrs. These spies would tell there generals that even though Sikhs were outnumbered and had less resources, their spirit and will to fight was unmatched. Sikhs never let innocent civilians die. They never attacked anyone who was running away from battle or anyone who surrendered. Sikhs never fought out of anger, revenge, or retaliation. The Mughal army was killing civilians, raping women, and torturing captured Sikhs. Sikhs never once committed any crimes against humanity during warfare. No matter what the enemy did, Guru Gobind Singh Ji always directed Sikhs to take the higher road.

During the battle of Chamkaur Sahib, the first Sikhs to attain shahadat in the battlefield were Bhai Kotha Singh Ji and Bhai Madan Singh Ji of village Bhagrana, in the district of Fatehgarh Sahib. The Sikhs in the fort would shoot arrows from the top. Five Sikhs went out at a time and fought in hand and hand combat. The goal was to the keep the enemy forces away from the fort. The battle waged on for hours, and the enemy forces fell down one by one.

The Request of Baba Ajit Singh Ji

Even at the young age of 17, Baba Ajit Singh Ji had also acquired top notch military acumen. Sikh history is filled with examples of Baba Ajit Singh Ji's superb leadership and command. Baba Ajit Singh Ji had already led many military operations. One of the cruel aspects about the government was that government officials would kidnap beautiful young women. This even happened at weddings. An official would come and kidnap the bride. Her parents and husband would remain helpless. The officials were backed by the government. Many of the girls who were kidnapped were very young teenagers. These girls had no voice and they were sexually abused

If the girls were non-Muslims, sometimes the ruthless government officials would justify kidnapping them in the name of Islam. They would say we are forcibly marrying these girls and they have been converted to Islam as a result. Of course, Islam does not allow such force. As we see over and over, such fanatics use religion as a guise. Once the girls were kidnapped, no one dared to stand up to the officials. Many just let their daughters go.

Once the Khalsa army rose, the cries of the young women were heard. The husbands and parents of the kidnapped girls would come to the Khalsa army, and the army would rescue the young women. Baba Ajit Singh Ji often led these rescue missions. One of his most famous was against Hakim Jabar Khan, who was known for kidnapping girls during their wedding processions. Sometimes, when the Khalsa army returned the girls home, their families would be afraid to keep them. Parents would worry that if they kept their daughters at home, they would face fierce repercussions from the government. The whole family could be in danger. Instead of going home, these women decided to live among the Sikhs. These women were welcomed into the Khalsa army. They were treated like daughters of the Khalsa.

Many times, Sikhs were so outnumbered that they would attack the enemy palaces to rescue the kidnapped girls at midnight, using the element of surprise to free these girls. This is where the common joke "Sardar ji de bara wajgaye," or "midnight has struck for the Sikh" originated. Guru Ji taught Sikhs "One woman is your rightful wife, and all others are to be seen as sisters, mothers, and daughters."[57] In this way, Sikhs have a heritage and a duty to treat all woman as they would want their sisters and daughters treated. They should respect all elder woman as their mothers.

My brothers, look at how Baba Ajit Singh Ji treated women. That is your mirror. Have you acted in a way that is worthy of a descendent of Baba Ajit Singh Ji. Do you protect vulnerable women when they are attacked, do you protect their reputations and treat them with dignity? Or are you the ones attacking their security and reputation. Do women feel safe with you. Look at the character of teenage Baba Ajit Singh Ji. You belong to that lineage. As Sikh sons, have you lived up to the honor of being called a brother of Baba Ajit Singh Ji.

As the battle raged and Sikhs started becoming shaheed, Sahibzada Ajit Singh Ji made a request to his father. He asked Guru Gobind Singh Ji if he could go and fight. Sahibzada Ajit Singh Ji had fought many battles before. However, this battle was different. This would be the last battle of Sahibzada Ajit Singh Ji. Each Sikh was fighting until shahadat. Baba Ajit Singh Ji would do the same.

Guru Gobind Singh Ji heard the request of Baba Ajit Singh Ji. Guru Ji remembered the very first time that Baba Ajit Singh Ji had ever picked up a sword. Guru Gobind Singh Ji had given Baba Ajit Singh Ji the sword for the first time and watched him fight with great pride. Guru Ji was proud that his young son was learning to fight against cruelty. Guru Gobind Singh Ji beamed with honor when Baba Ajit Singh Ji picked up weapons and learned to fight for the first time.

---

[57] " Eka nari jati hoye par nari dhee bhain vakhaanai"- Vaaran Bhai Gurdas Ji, Panna 6, Pauri 8

Today, Guru Ji would glow with even greater honor once more as he watched his eldest son fought for the last time.

Guru Gobind Singh Ji was thankful that his son was ready to give his life fighting against cruelty. Guru Ji gave Baba Ajit Singh Ji weopons and stood at the top of the fort and as he watched his son fight, Guru Ji's chest filled with pride. Today his son had conquered the greatest enemy, death. The name Ajit means one who is undefeated. Everyone dies one day, but few become shaheed. To welcome death fearlessly, to sacrifice yourself for good, that is a privilege not many are given.

On the battlefield, Baba Ajit Singh Ji first fought with the sword. The battle was fierce, and swords clashed so much that Baba Ajit Singh Ji's sword soon broke. Baba Ajit Singh Ji then pulled out a weapon called the barshee, (a spear like weapon). The last weapon Baba Ajit Singh Ji pulled out was a called a Khanjar (a small knife-like weapon). The enemy shot at Baba Ajit Singh Ji's body with a storm of arrows and bullets. Baba Ajit Singh Ji's body was covered in arrows and pierced with bullets, yet he fought till his last breath. According to historical sources, Baba Ajit Singh Ji did not fall to the ground and become shaheed. Baba Ajit Singh Ji became shaheed first, and then fell to the ground. He fought till the last second.

Guru Gobind Singh Ji watched his son fight and screamed words of encouragement. Poet Santokh Singh Ji describes Baba Ajit Singh Ji as a crocodile. Just like a crocodile makes waves anytime they move in the water, each time Baba Ajit Singh Ji turned, he made waves taking down enemy soldiers. As arrows penetrated the body of Baba Ajit

Singh Ji, Guru Gobind Singh Ji shouted jaikaras[58] from the top of the fort. It was a sight never before seen in history. A child's body is being pierced with weapons, and a father is smiling and telling the child, "Good job". Leaders are quick to start wars for other people's children to fight in, yet it is unheard of for a leader to send their own child into the battlefield, that too in a situation where shahadat was imminent. That is the heart of Guru Gobind Singh Ji, who sacrificed his biological family for the family of creation, who raised children, biological and disciple, so strong that they look death in the eyes and death trembles before them. We should be proud to be from this family.

You will Steer the Boat of the Panth.

After the martyrdom of Baba Ajit Singh Ji, Baba Jujhar Singh Ji came to Guru Gobind Singh Ji and asked if he could also go out and fight. The thirteen-year-old fearless son of the Guru said "Father, it is my turn to become shaheed." Guru Gobind Singh Ji hugged his one remaining son tightly against his chest and said "Today you have me the proudest I have ever been of you. By coming to me yourself and asking me if you can join the battle, you have started a new tradition. After you many Jujharoos (warriors) will come jumping into the battlefield when needed. I did not have to ask you; you came to me ready to give shahadat."

Guru Gobind Singh Ji lovingly got his son ready for his battle, for his shahadat. Guru Ji gave Baba Jujhar Singh Ji small weapons and tied his small cummerbund. Guru Gobind Singh Ji looked at his son and said, *"I am giving you a khanjar (small knife-like weapon), consider this a large*

---

[58] This is the Sikh battle slogan and is said out of joy. It means "Those who reply are blessed." The reply is "Sat Sri Akal," meaning "truth never dies."

sword, I am giving you a nejha (harpoon like weapon), consider this the arrow of your grandfather." Guru Ji continued and said, *"you may be stabbed many times, you may be shot by arrows, but my life, my child, remember, if you get hurt do not wince, don't even let the word "ow" come out of your mouth."*

Guru Gobind Singh Ji then said to his dear son *"Go and fight, I surrender you to the Creator. Fight and be killed, I surrender you to the Creator. Do not forget God, I surrender you to the Creator. Keep Sikhi alive, I surrender you to the Creator."* Guru Gobind Singh Ji prayed, *"When you are in the battle, May God give you strength. May God give you the blessing of shahadat."* Guru Gobind Singh Ji sent Baba Jujhar Singh Ji on the path of his brother and told him, *"It was always my desire since you were born for my eyes to see you fight with the sword and take the blow of the barshee to your chest for the sake of righteousness."*

Before Baba Jujhar Singh Ji left, Guru Gobind Singh Ji told him that *"My son, you are the navigator, the one who with steer the ship of the Khalsa panth. Go, lay down your life, sacrifice your head so that the boat can move forward."* Today, these powerful words belong to all young Sikhs. Guru Gobind Singh Ji is telling Baba Jujhar Singh Ji that with your sacrifice, the ideology of Guru Nanak Dev Ji will thrive in this world. Guru Ji is telling his child to give his life so that Sikhi will survive. The message of Sikhi is so precious that it is worth more to Guru Gobind Singh Ji than his own life, and even his son's life. Today, we are the ones chosen to safeguard this message. We all have the responsibility to keep the message of Sikhi alive. We have the responsibility to keep the tradition of fighting cruelty alive. We are all captains on the boat of the Khalsa movement. We must ask ourselves if we are sinking the boat of Guru Nanak Dev Ji or if we are fighting to steer it forward.

79

It took seconds on the battlefield for Baba Jujhar Singh Ji to attain shahadat. He followed his older brother's footsteps. Blessed is Guru Gobind Singh Ji, who gave everything he had for the Khalsa Panth. Blessed is the heart that surrendered everything to God. Blessed is the kind heart, the fierce heart, the deep heart, the loving heart, of Guru Gobind Singh Ji.

I Belong to the Khalsa.

By the end of the night, out of 40 Sikhs, there were five left, alongside Guru Gobind Singh Ji. Bhai Daya Singh Ji, Bhai Dharam Singh Ji, Bhai Sant Singh Ji, Bhai Sangat Singh Ji and Bhai Maan Singh Ji were the only Sikhs left. These five Sikhs made a decision. They decided they were going to overrule Guru Gobind Singh Ji. Guru Gobind Singh Ji always gave the panth the authority to overrule and command him. This was the right of the panth, of the five beloved gursikhs. Guru Gobind Singh Ji, in a revolutionary move, gave the panth the ability to override the Guru's decisions. This example of a Guru giving his disciples this power had never before been seen in history. Even the very fact that Guru Gobind Singh Ji had five gursikhs give him Amrit had never been seen before. Blessed is Guru Gobind Singh Ji who put his disciples above everything, even himself. No wonder they say that there is no generous giver like Guru Gobind Singh ji and there is no beggar like the Guru.

When Guru Gobind Singh Ji gave the Khalsa the right to baptize him, it was revolutionary. No Saint had ever taken baptism from their devotees. It was always the saints who gave baptism. This was unheard of. This level of checks and balances existed for Sikhs in 1704, even before the first democracy was ever established. There is one incident where Guru Gobind Singh Ji was walking with his Sikhs. There was the grave of a Saint. Guru Gobind Singh Ji touched the grave with his sword, in an act of reverence. Bhai Daya Singh Ji told Guru Gobind Singh Ji that this was against the teachings of Gurbani and that Guru Gobind Singh Ji was in violation. Guru Gobind Singh Ji hugged Bhai Daya Singh Ji and said, you have made me happy. I now know the Khalsa army is ready to rule themselves. They are not afraid to question the truth. They put the teachings above the teacher. Even after giving up his whole family for the Khalsa, Guru Gobind Singh Ji still writes that he will forever bow and be subservient to the love of the Khalsa. Let us also become Khalsa in our hearts. Let us also enjoy this love of the Guru.

The beloved Gursikhs told Guru Gobind Singh Ji that he was to leave the fort. This was an order. Guru Gobind Singh Ji said how can you ask me to leave? And that too at night? That is a job for thieves. The five beloveds said, "say what you will, but this is an order of the panth." Guru Gobind Singh Ji agreed under some conditions. The first condition was that Guru Gobind Singh Ji would not leave in secret like a thief. Guru Ji wanted it to be announced with the drum that he was going. Guru Ji had Bhai Sant Singh Ji sound the drum as he clapped loudly and announced "Guru Gobind Singh, the Guru of the Sikhs is leaving this fort. If anyone has the bravery, come and capture him." Two Sikhs were to stay in the fort and everyone else would leave. According to history, there was a fight here and each Sikh told the other that you should leave and survive, I will stay and face shahadat. This was the love and fearlessness that they had for each other.

Finally, it was decided that Bhai Sangat Singh Ji and Bhai Sant Singh Ji would stay. Bhai Sant Singh Ji was to keep the drum, the nagara, sounding. The nagara drum is a symbol of a sovereign and independent people. It is the symbol of freedom. For this reason, Guru Gobind Singh Ji made sure that the drum stayed beating. As long as even one

Sikh is alive, the nagara beat should go on. Guru Gobind Singh Ji also gave Bhai Sangat Singh Ji his *kalgi*, the feather shaped ornament which he wore on his turban. This symbolizes royalty. He told Bhai Sant Singh Ji to keep the battle going and to stand at the top of the fort and keep shooting arrows. That way, even though there were few Sikhs, the battle would go on till no Sikhs were left standing. This symbolizes that as long as there is life, the fight for righteousness should continue.

Both the Nagara and the Kalgi are gifts which Guru Gobind Singh Ji gave the panth, the ability to live with royalty, sovereignty, and independence, the ability to hold your head high. Guru Gobind Singh Ji took people who were outcasts and taught them that they are royal and precious. They are free and independent. Guru Gobind Singh Ji gave everyone the realization that as children of God, we are all divine and have the right to live with dignity. Every human has this right.

Do you have Cloth for all my Children?

After shouting jaikaras, and making it known to the enemy that he was leaving, Guru Gobind Singh Ji left Chamkaur Sahib alongside Bhai Daya Singh Ji, Bhai Maan Singh Ji, and Bhai Dharam Singh Ji. Guru Gobind Singh Ji walked barefoot so that he would not step with his shoes on the bodies or *kesh*[59] of his beloved gursikhs. On the way, Guru Ji and the Sikhs passed the bodies of Baba Ajit Singh Ji and Baba Jujhar Singh Ji. Bhai Daya Singh Ji ripped his

---

[59] Kesh refers here to the long uncut hair of the Sikhs. Sikhs believe that the creator made our bodies perfectly and lovingly. For that reason, Sikhs stay close to nature and their natural form. This includes not cutting hair and not getting piercings. For a Sikh, they should clean and decorate their body, but they should not alter their form. In many religions, uncut hair is considered to be indicative of spirituality.

turban in two pieces, gave it to Guru Gobind Singh Ji and said, *"Use this cloth to cover the bodies of your sons, they have no coffins."* Guru Gobind Singh Ji said, "Every single Sikh is my child. None of them have coffins. Do you have enough cloth for all my children?" Guru Gobind Singh Ji told Bhai Daya Singh Ji, "Keep your turban. Shaheed's don't need coffins." They are govered under the cloth of the star filled sky. Guru Gobind Singh Ji left, leaving the bodies of all his sons uncovered. The bodies lay there in the cold. Guru Gobind Singh Ji left in the dark cold night, after sacrificing everything.

The Bed of Thorns of my Beloved is the Best.

Guru Gobind Singh Ji left Chamkaur Sahib and spent the frigid night sleeping in the dark and thick Machiware Jungle. This was a night like no other, the night after Guru Gobind Singh Ji gave up his sons, his Sikhs, his family, his comforts, and home at Anandpur Sahib. Instead of a warm bed with blankets, in the middle of the December cold, Guru Gobind Singh Ji slept on the bare ground, with nothing but rocks and thorns as his bed and pillows. Guru Ji's body was severly injured. The one thing Guru Gobind Singh Ji did have was the comfort of knowing that he kept his faith, he served God, and that God was pleased with him. In this condition, Guru Gobind Singh Ji wrote a prayer thanking God for this. The English translation of this prayer is as follows:

"Would someone tell my beloved friend God the state of his disciples,

Without you God, warm blankets are like a disease, and living in a comfortable house is like living with snakes.

Without you, fancy flasks are like spikes, and costly cups are like daggers,

Separation from you feels painful, like being slaughtered by a butcher

This thorn bed of my beloved friend is the best

If God is not with me, every pleasure feels like I am burning in a furnace."[60]

Just months ago, Guru Gobind Singh Ji had riches and elephants. Guru Gobind Singh Ji had an elephant named Parsadi who would wave fans and do seva. Guru Gobind Singh Ji had a beautiful family and beloved Sikhs surrounding him. There was the love and laughter of Anandpur Sahib. Today, that Guru is sleeping on a cold floor after losing his whole family. Still that Guru thanks God and has no regrets. For Sikhs, there is no such thing as "Sog" (despair). Whether it is a birthday or funeral, Sikhs will always read the prayer of bliss (Anand Sahib) and always eat sweet parsad (sweet offering which is given out after every Sikh prayer service). Traditionally, sweets are not eaten during times of mourning and sadness. However, a Sikh never mourns. No matter the tragedy, there will never be a Sikh ceremony where sweet prasad is not eaten or Anand Sahib is not read. This is the spirit of chardi kala (boundless optimism which comes from faith in God's plan) that our Guru gave us. A Sikh always trusts God's will and surrenders to the creator. A Sikh trusts the journey and rejoices in all that Waheguru Ji does. The word "sog" is not in a Sikhs vocabulary.

---

[60] *"Mittar pyare noon"*-Dasam Bani, 711

A Brave Young Girl Becomes the Final Shaheed of Chamkaur Sahib.

Bhai Sangat Singh Ji and Bhai Sant Singh Ji stayed in the fort, and kept the nagara beating and the arrows flying, till their last breath. Seeing the kalgi, the enemy forces thought that Bhai Sangat Singh Ji was Guru Gobind Singh Ji, and that maybe they were tricked. They chopped off the head of Bhai Sangat Singh Ji and brought it to the government. That is when they realized that it was the head of a Gursikh and not of the Guru. Bhai Sangat Singh Ji and the Sikhs of Chamkaur Sahib teach us that each Sikh should be so much like their Guru, through their character, their glow, and their virtue, that even enemies see the Guru in them.

The enemy forces went village to village saying that they had captured Chamkaur Sahib. A brave 16-year-old girl from the village Khroond, named Bibi Harsharan Kaur Ji, heard this and snuck out at night to give the bodies of the Sikh soldiers a proper cremation. She was able to build a pyre and had cremated the bodies of both sahibzaday, and 30 Sikhs, including her husband Bhai Pritam Singh Ji, before she was caught. Bibi Harsharan Kaur was able to fight and kill many enemy soldiers before they stabbed her and threw her in the funeral pyre to be burned alive.

PART THREE:
THE NIGHT OF 9 POH
GURUDWARA KOTWALI SAHIB

Police Brutality towards Mother Gujri Ji and the Sahibzaday

The police were ecstatic when they found out that Mother Gujri and the sahibzaday were captured. They tortured the sahibzaday and Mother Gujri Ji mercilessly. According to eyewitness Bhai Doona Singh Handooria, Mata Ji and the sahibzaday were put in sacks and thrown in a horse drawn prison carriage. They had chili peppers put in their eyes and were beaten. They were tortured in the prison of Morinda and kept cold and hungry. They slept on the bare ground. The government did not want to execute Mother Gujri Ji and the sahibzaday. That would be a loss for them. They wanted Mother Gujri Ji and the sahibzaday to bow before them. They wanted Mother Gujri Ji and the Sahibzaday to be scared. It would have been a huge victory for the tyrants if the children of Guru Gobind Singh Ji embraced Islam and bowed down to the government. This would end the Sikh movement right there. The Sahibzaday and Mother Gujri's struggle was the Sikh struggle. If they failed this test, we would not have Sikhi. They represented all of us. For this reason, every effort was made to terrify and brutally torture Mother Gujri and the Sahibzaday, so that they would leave their faith and the ideology of Guru Nanak Dev Ji would be finished.

Finding Freedom Behind Bars

The night of 9th Poh, Mother Gujri and the sahibzaday were in a prison cell. The bars of the prison are still there today. If one listens with their heart, listens in the language of Bhaakhiya Bhau Apaar,[61] they can hear the bars speak. These bars tell a story. A story about a dream. A story about freedom. A story of the pure souls who blessed this dark and terrifying prison cell. Mother Gujri Ji is the first Sikh women who ever had to face torture in police custody, and who had to face imprisonment in a cold and dingy cell. However, Mother Gujri Ji was not the last, and she remains an inspiration to all women who are imprisoned for challenging cruelty, and for doing the right thing.

In Sikhi, freedom has nothing to do with the body. It has everything to do with the spirit. A person can be physically free but mentally a prisoner. A person can be rich and live in western democratic nations, yet still be a slave. Slavery is mental not physical. If a person cares what other people think, they are a slave. If a person is afraid of death, they are a slave. If a person cannot control their greed, they are a slave. If a person cannot control their lust, they are a slave. All these things control the way a person acts, thus controlling their consequences. Likewise, a person can be physically enslaved but mentally free.

It is possible to enslave the body of a true Sikh, but it is not possible to enslave a true Sikh's spirit. Guru Gobind Singh Ji gave Sikhs the identity of being free and sovereign, no matter what. There was an old expression saying a Sikh is always either a *baagi* (rebel) or a *baadshah* (king). However, this is inaccurate. A Sikh is always a king even when they are a rebel. They are always free and royal, even when they are in jail. This is because a Sikh's royalty does not come from riches or power. It comes from the awareness that they are a child of the divine Creator. It comes from the identity given to Sikhs by Guru Gobind Singh Ji. It comes

---

[61] The language of infinite love. According to Gurbani, this is the language of God.

from the inner connection with the most powerful king of the Universe. Gurbani says *"There is no king equal to God. The kings of the world last for four days (are temporary), as they run their kingdoms with falsehood."*[62]

Guru Gobind Singh Ji uplifted helpless people who had been persecuted and abused their whole lives. Poor and low caste people, those who were exploited and stomped on, people who were treated like worthless garbage- Guru Gobind Singh Ji loved and cared for those people. Those who had been judged and condemned and called low, Guru Gobind Singh Ji made them realize that they were no loss than kings and queens. This made some of the high castes and elites jealous. They would even throw things and physically attack Sikhs who were going to Anandpur Sahib. The elites felt jealous that the same people we kept under our feet for years, those people are walking around with their heads held high. Society had told these people that they are low caste nobodies. Guru Gobind Singh Ji told them they were the light of God. Even now Guru Granth Sahib Ji says that the Guru stands with those who have nothing and no one. Gurbani says "Those who not only low but are the considered lowest of low (category/caste), the bottom of the very bottom, Guru Nanak is with them always."[63] This is what scared the government the most. People who had been put down for centuries were no longer subservient. They realized their worth. They were no longer afraid and thus could no longer be enslaved. This freedom was given to them by Sikhi.

The point of putting the sahibzaday and Mother Gujri in Jail was to scare them; to punish and terrorize them. The rulers wanted to scare Guru Gobind Singh Ji's mother and

---

[62] Guru Granth Sahib Ji, 856
[63] Guru Granth Sahib Ji,

young children so that they would comply with the government. The government thought that this would demoralize the followers of Sikhi. The government tried every form of torture to break their resolve. It is only those who bow down before God that can stall tall before even the most powerful rulers.

The sahibzaday and Mother Gujri are sitting in a cell, yet their spirit is free. They have a dream, a dream for the world. A dream for the future. A dream that they fight for in the jail cell. A dream that they will give their lives for in the brick wall of Sirhind. A dream for humanity to live free from fear. A dream for a world where all are equal. A dream for a world where all are loved and cared for. The dream of Guru Nanak Dev Ji, the dream of *Halimee Raj*, the kingdom of compassion. When Jewish mothers used to put their children to bed, before the days of Isreal, they would tell their children that when they open their eyes they will be in a free land. This put the spirit of independence in them. Likewise, Sikh elders have put the spirit of *raj karega khalsa* (the pure of heart will rule) inside every Sikh, when we do ardas.

Even the symbols that the Guru's gave the Sikhs are symbols of a free and sovereign people. The nagara or the battle drum was only allowed to play in the Kings army. Aurangzeb forbade anyone else, other than himself, to beat the nagara. Aurungzeb's own son was not even allowed to beat the nagara when he won battles. When Aurangzeb's son, Bahadur Shah, was victorious in the Battle of Multan, Bahadur Shah celebrated by beating the nagara. This upset Aurangzeb, and Aurangzeb told Bahdur Shah that only the king can beat the nagara. The Sikhs kept the nagara beating during every battle. This symbolizes that the Sikhs are royal and sovereign. Likewise, the Nishan sahib, the Sikh flag, and the throne of Akal Thakat are all indicative of a free people. Enslaved people cannot have their own flag. Each

Gurudwara is its own state within a state. Guru Gobind Singh Ji prepared the Sikhs to be a free entity. It is a Punjabi tradition that before a child is born a grandmother will stitch a sweater for the baby in anticipation. This happens when the baby is in the womb. In the same way, when the Khalsa was in its infancy, Guru Gobind Singh Ji gave us the Nishan sahib and the nagara, as symbols of hope that one day the Khalsa will not only give freedom to others, but they too will live free. Today, the sahibzaday sit in jail for our freedom. They bear torture so that one day tyranny can be eradicated. They stand up and keep the gift of Sikhi intact, so that future generations can find bliss and freedom through the Guru's teachings.

Today, we must ask ourselves if we are free. When a person is enslaved, their way of speaking changes, and they do not speak their mind. They flatter others. Their way of wearing clothes and the food they eat changes. Their language changes. This happens often when a free country becomes a colony. Today it is important that Sikhs preserve their customs, spirit, and the language of Gurmukhi. As Sikhs spread out around the world, we must realize that Gurmukh is not merely our mother language. Today, Sikh mothers are born all around the world. A mother's language can be English, or Spanish, or French. However, the language of Gurbani is Gurmukhi. Gurmukhi is the language which turns our face toward the Guru. It connects us to the Guru's words. When a Sikh fails to understand Guru Granth Sahib Ji, then it is difficult for them to follow Sikhi. While translations are a welcome beginning, there are many words which are difficult to translate and much of the meaning gets lost. The essence of Gurbani is best felt by learning Gurmukhi. Today, people of Sikh heritage are doing well financially, however we have lost the connection to Gurbani, and thus our mentality becomes that of one who is enslaved. We have lost our uniqueness, and our mission. We have lost our fearlessness and we have become greedy for the world. Even while living in western democracies, our bodies are free but mentally we are slaves. It is by remembering the brave and free spirit of the sahibzaday, our brothers, that our chains are broken, and we live as our true free selves.

The Cowardly Masands Turn their Back on the Guru

Guru Gobind Singh Ji, Bhai Daya Singh Ji, Bhai Dharam Singh Ji, and Bhai Maan Singh Ji had planned to meet using the stars as navigation. The three gursikhs were able to find each other but soon it was sunrise, and they could not find Guru Gobind Singh Ji. They did ardas and said a prayer. After this prayer, they saw the sun reflected off of Guru Gobind Singh Ji's *gulshatraan* (A protective covering which is used for the thumb when shooting arrows). This gulshatraan was given to Guru Gobind Singh Ji as a gift and it had a diamond in it. Guru Gobind Singh Ji had blisters and cuts on his feet and history says Guru Ji was so injured that Bhai Daya Singh Ji had to support him on his shoulders so that Guru Ji could walk to the river and drink water.

After spending the night in Macchiware, Guru Gobind Singh Ji went to the house of two former masands named Gulaba and Punjaba. Guru Ji reached their house the night of 9th Poh. The masands however were scared for their lives and did not want Guru Gobind Singh Ji to stay with him. This shows that just calling oneself a Sikh does not make a person a Sikh. These former masands had not reached the state of fearlessness. They valued their lives more than their conscience. They were people of the world. Belonging to a religion alone means nothing. It is a person's inner state which matters.

PART FOUR: THE NIGHT OF 10TH POH AT THANDA BURJ, GURUDWARA FATEHGARH SAHIB

Who are these Small Children under the Peepal tree?

The saintly mother and precious sons of the guru were kept in the most inhumane conditions. However, no amount of torment could shake the immense faith and unwavering courage of the young princes. En route from Morinda to Sirhind, the horse drawn prison cart carrying Mother Gujri Ji and the sahibzaday briefly stopped. Mother Ji and the sahibzaday were kept in a closed wooden cart, just in case Gursikhs saw them and tried to free them. Many people gathered around Mother Gujri Ji and the young princes. They cried out in shock at the extent of the Mughal Government's depravity. They wondered why an elderly woman and two small children were being agonized and tortured with such brutality. Sikh Historian and eyewitness, Doona Singh Handooria describes the reaction of onlookers in his work, Katha Guru Ke Santaan Kee, by saying, "*Jaye Sirhind jab he tab aan so peepal hayth bithaiye. Pooch rahe yeh kaun so balak tohe so goadee mehi kehi chupaiye. (On the way to Sirhind, Mother Gujjar Kaur Ji and the Sahibzaday were seated beneath a pippala (sacred fig) tree. Onlookers came and asked, who are these small children that you hold tightly in your lap, (wrapped up securely to protect from them the bitter cold)?*"

Onlookers cursed the government and their cruelty. Hindus, Muslims, and Sikhs came together in mercy and love. Guru Hargobind Sahib Ji had once visited Sirhind. There were Sikhs there at the time of the sahibzaday's shaheedee. The crowd saluted the bravery of Guru Gobind Singh Jis kind children and selfless mother. Those Sikhs, Hindus, and Muslims who had humane hearts tried to save Mother Gujri and the Sahibzaday. They got together and offered to pay the weight in gold of Mother Gujri and Sahibzaday, in order to set them free. They knew that the ruthless governor of Sirhind, Wazir Khan (Wajeeda) would not spare even the innocent children of Guru Gobind Singh Ji. The government refused to take their offer. It is from here that Mother Gujjar Kaur Ji and the Sahibzaday were taken to Thanda Burj Sahib. Today there is a Gurudwara in the place called *Rath Sahib*.

Guru Gobind Singh Ji's Muslim Children.

On one hand, Gulaba and Punjaba, people claiming to be Sikhs turned Guru Gobind Singh Ji away. On the other hand, Muslim devotees of Guru Gobind Singh Ji, brothers Ghani Khan and Nabhi Khan came and requested Guru Gobind Singh Ji to come to their house. On the way, Guru Gobind Singh Ji visited Mother Har Daye Kaur. She was a devotee of Guru Gobind Singh Ji and would make clothes for him. Each day she would pray that Guru Gobind Singh Ji would come and wear the outfit that she made him. The types of clothes she made were very difficult and she worked very hard and lovingly. Guru Gobind Singh Ji reached her house and honored her love. Guru Gobind Singh Ji blessed Mother Jee and took the garment. Love has a great power. It is like a magnet. Gurbani teaches that everything may be in God's power, but God is in the power of those who love him. [64]

By inviting Guru Gobind Singh Ji to their house, Ghani Khan and Nabhi Khan were risking their lives and the lives of their family, including their small children. Guru Gobind Singh Ji did not want to put their lives at risk, so Guru Ji donned the clothes of a Muslim Saint (pir). Guru Ji took the garment that Mother Har Daye Kaur gave him and dyed it blue (the color worn by Muslim pirs). When Ghani Khan and Nabhi Khan were asked by authorities who Guru Gobind Singh Ji was, they said he is "Uch da pir", which means two things. Uch is a city where long haired pirs were found. Uch

---

[64] Guru Granth Sahib Ji, 962

also means the highest pir. For Ghani Khan and Nabhi Khan, Guru Gobind Singh Ji was their Uch da pir. He was their highest saint.

Ghani Khan and Nabhi Khan put their lives at risk to spend time with their guru. Truth and love have no religion. Guru Gobind Singh Ji wrote a hukamnama stating *"Ghani Khan and Nabhi Khan are my children, they are my offspring, and my Jigar de tukray*[65] Guru Gobind Singh Ji wrote this down as a *hukamnama* (official order). This hukamnama is still preserved in Gurudwara Ghani Khan Nabhi Khan. There is no example in the whole universe like this. At the same time that the younger sahibzaday were being tortured by Wazir Khan, Guru Gobind Singh Ji is embracing two Khans, loving them, and officially adopting them as his children. Guru Ji even uses the term *"Jigar de tukray"* for them. This teaches that there are good and bad people in every community and religious labels mean nothing. It is love and character which make a person belong to the family of Guru Gobind Singh Ji and not a mere religious label. Likewise, being born a Sikh does not make one a Sikh. It is impossible to be born a Sikh. It is actions that make one a Sikh and bring one close to the Guru.

Dr. Balbir Singh (Brother of Bhai Vir Singh Ji) Ji writes that there was a little girl in the house of Ghani Khan and Nabhi Khan. She was one of their daughters. When this little girl found out that Guru Gobind Singh Ji had adopted her father, she jumped with joy. She asked, "Does that mean I am your poatee (paternal granddaughter)?" She then started jumping in excitement and started singing, I am your granddaughter, I am your granddaughter, your beloved pearl, your granddaughter." There is no end to how many hearts

_____

[65] A word of endearment usually used for one's children. Means a piece of my heart.

97

were touched by the delightful love of Guru Gobind Singh Ji. Everywhere Guru Ji went, he poured love onto others like rain on dry jungle plants.

The First Night in the Cold Tower

In order to torture Mother Gujri Ji and the younger sahibzaday, they were kept in the cold tower, or *Thanda Burj*. They were kept hungry and not given any warm clothes. Eyewitness Doona Singh Handooria Ji writes about the grave and callous torment that was inflicted on these 7- and 9-year-old princes. Handooria Ji writes that Baba Zorawar Singh Ji and Baba Fateh Singh Ji were tied to a tree and had stones pelted at them. One stone directly hit the right eye of Baba Fateh Singh Ji. They were then asked to convert to Islam. Baba Fateh Singh Ji wiped the blood from his eye and said "never." As a punishment for greeting Wazir Khan with "Waheguru Ji Ka Khalsa, Waheguru Ji Ki Fateh", Baba Zorawar Singh Ji and Baba Fateh Singh Ji were whipped with horse whips until their small bodies were drenched in blood.

Mother Gujri spent the whole night telling the sahibzaday about her beloved husband, Guru Teg Bahadur Ji. Twenty-nine years had passed since the shahadat of Mother Gujri Ji's deeply loved soulmate. However, Mother Gujri Ji never forgot Guru Teg Bahadur Ji and she told her sweet grandchild about their brave grandfather. Yesterday, Mother Gujri Ji sat at this place with her two beloved grandchildren. Today, she is sitting among us. She is sitting with thousands of her beloved grandchildren. We are all sitting in her lap and hearing the history of our ancestors. This history gave the sahibzaday the courage to face evil, torture, and death. This history has the power to also give us that courage if we open our hearts. Mother Gujri Ji please also give us strength to overcome our difficulties. Pray for us too. Teach us like you taught Baba Zorawar Singh Ji and Baba Fateh Singh Ji. We are also yours, love us too. There is evil all around us. May we join our brothers in the fight and have the courage to be candles in the darkness. May their light live in us, never to be extinguished.

There were many towers, but Thanda Burj was the tallest and the coldest at 140 feet. The Hansla river ran near the tower and hit against it. The wind from the river made the tower especially cold. In the summer, this was where royals would go to escape the summer heat before the invention of air conditioners. Cool air constantly blew into the tower. In the winter the bitter cold was unbearable. There was a well inside the tower which made it even colder. December was the coldest month of the year. The heartless tyrants kept the small children and elderly mother in this tower without any food, water, or warm clothing. They wanted badly to break their resolve. It would have been a trophy to convert the mother and children of Guru Gobind Singh Ji to Islam. Today, as we sit in our blankets and coats, each time we feel the cold wind, we should remember those small, vulnerable, tender bodies who took such pain upon themselves. They must have turned blue and shivered in the bitter cold. The whole night must have been torture for them. We should think of our parents and grandparents and how we protect their feeble bodies from the cold. We should think of our children and how we make sure they bundle up in layers each winter. All the Sahibzaday had to do to be free from this torture was to give up their faith. We must never forget their sacrifices.

Wazir Khan, the sinful Wajeeda, was the governor of this district and Chamkaur Sahib. He was filled with rage because he had tried so hard to stop the Sikhs, yet his efforts failed. First his government did not capture Guru Gobind Singh Ji at Anandpur Sahib, even by sending all their troops and surrounding the fort for 8 months. Then the government was not able to capture Guru Gobind Singh Ji at Chamkaur Sahib, despite the Sikhs being incredibly outnumbered. After failing miserably in this aspect, Wazir Khan now had the children of Guru Gobind Singh Ji in his custody. This was a win for his damaged ego. By torturing Mother Gujri Ji and the sahibzaday, Wajeeda is trying to find inner peace. All the comforts we have are comforts that our ancestors sacrificed, so that we don't have to face the pain that they faced. If we want to be able to look Baba Zorawar Singh Ji and Baba Fateh Singh Ji in the eyes, we must live up to the identity our ancestors fought to bless us with. Before all else, greater than any other affiliation, we are brothers and sisters of Baba Ajit Singh Ji, Baba Jujhar Singh Ji, Baba Zorawar Singh Ji, Baba Fateh Singh Ji.

The Kindness of Baba Moti Ram Mehra Ji

Today we remember the kindness of Baba Moti Ram Mehra Ji, who snuck into Thanda Burj to give the Sahibzaday warm milk. Baba Moti Mehra Ji, a devotee of Guru Gobind Singh Ji, was blessed with a pure conscience and a deep love for the guru. Baba Moti Mehra Ji risked everything to feed Mother Gujri Ji and the Sahibzaday warm milk. Baba Mothi Mehra Ji's mother's name was Bibi Ladho Ji, and his father's name was Bhai Hara Ram Ji. Bhai Hara Ram Ji was also shaheed. Baba Moti Mehra Ji's wife, Bibi Bholi Ji, was a compassionate devotee of Guru Gobind Singh Ji. Baba Moti Mehra Ji and Bibi Bholi Ji also had a seven-year-old son named Bhai Naraina Ji. They lived in a place called Mansoori Tibba, Sirhind.

The government had announced that if anybody tried to help the family of the Guru, they would be punished brutally along with their families. However, Bibi Ladho Ji and the family of Moti Ram Ji could not eat or drink anything knowing the precious innocent children of Guru Gobind Singh Ji were being kept hungry in the Thanda Burj. Baba Moti Mehra Ji sold all the jewelry in his house, and even sold his house, to bribe the guards who were posted at Thanda Burj. Baba Moti Ram Ji was able to successfully bribe the guards, the dishonest employees of a dishonest regime, to let him secretly go in the Thanda Burj and serve Mother Gujri Ji and the young sahibzaday a glass of warm milk.

Sewa, selfless service, is not measured by how much you give; it is measured by the feeling in your heart. In terms of quantity, a glass of milk may not be considered a lot. However, there was so much love behind that glass of milk that Baba Moti Mehra Ji risked his whole family's life to offer it. On one hand there is Gangu, who may have given more to the sahibzaday and Mother Gujri Ji in terms of quantity. Gangu gave them a meal, a bed to sleep in, a roof over their heads, etc. Before this, Gangu worked as a cook in the Guru's house and served there. However, Gangu's heart was full of greed and deceit. There was no love so his seva was not accepted. Baba Moti Ram Mehra Ji's glass of milk is greater than Gangu's lifetime of "sewa". The Guru's scale is different than human scales. In Sikhi it is feeling and quality which matters, not quantity. Bhai Gurdas Ji states *"If a devotee gives even a shell[66] (Cowdee) with love to the Guru, in return the Guru will bless them with every single treasure."*[67] No sewa is small in the Guru's house, if it is done with love and sincerity.

All three days that Mother Gujri Ji and the sahibzaday were kept in the Thanda Burj, Baba Moti Ram Mehra Ji lovingly brought them milk. Mother Gujri gave her blessing to Baba Moti Ram Mehra Ji. Poet, Bhai Prem Ji, said that

---

[66] A Cowdee was a very low form of currency, less than a penny.
[67] Vaaran Bhai Gurdas Ji, 111

this blessing was worth more to Baba Moti Ram Mehra Ji than all other precious things of the world. All worldly treasures were worthless before the treasure of Mother Gujri Ji's blessing. Indeed, Bhai Moti Ram Mehra Ji gave up everything to obtain this priceless blessing. Just as Guru Gobind Singh Ji sacrificed his family and said, "It is okay if I lose everything, may my Sikhs prosper," the devotees of Guru Gobind Singh Ji sacrificed everything in the love of the Guru.

Baba Moti Ram Mehra Ji, Bibi Ladho Ji, Bibi Bholi Ji, and even their seven-year-old son, Bhai Naraina Ji, were mercilessly executed by being crushed alive in the oil mill. Their only crime was serving the innocent elderly mother and pure children of Guru Gobind Singh Ji warm milk. One by one, the whole family was murdered in the oil mill. Their innocent blood, their pure kind righteous blood, spilled out into the big pan that was used to collect the oil. The family's flesh and muscles were turned into marrow and their bones were crushed to powder. They refused to repent for their actions and proudly accepted shahadat. The glasses that Baba Moti Ram Mehra Ji gave Mother Gujri Ji and the Sahibzaday milk in are still preserved at Gurudwara Moti Ram Mehra Ji, near Gurdwara Fatehgarh Sahib. When Baba Banda Singh Bahadur Ji heard of Baba Moti Ram Mehra Ji's sacrifice, he said the famous quote, "Blessed is Baba Moti Raam Mehra Ji, who did a great deed by serving the beloveds of Guru Gobind Singh Ji milk." When remembering the shaheeds of Poh 1704, it is important to never forget shaheed Moti Ram Mehra Ji, Shaheed Bibi Ladho Ji, Shaheed Bibi Bholi Ji, and Shaheed Bhai Naraina Ji.

Mother Gujri Ji Prepares her Beloved Grandchildren for Court

Mother Gujri Ji sat in the tower with her beloved grandchildren. She prepared them for what was to come. Mother Gujri Ji put Baba Zorawar Singh Ji and Baba Fateh Singh Ji in her lap and told them about their heritage. She prepared them to bear the torture that would be inflicted on their young bodies. Today, in our times of pain we should remember Mother Gujri Ji and Thanda Burj. Just as Mother Gujri Ji prepared Baba Zorawar Singh Ji and Baba Fateh Singh Ji for their test, Mother Gujri Ji will help us succeed through all our trials and tribulations. Just as a degree comes with examinations, spiritually, we cannot progress without tests. Each second, a Sikhs life is full of tests and trials. These tests make us stronger. Baba Zorawar Singh Ji and Baba Fateh Singh Ji went through the labor of a difficult test, but it is our kaum that obtained the fruit of their labor. When we pray, it is as if we are sitting in class learning theory. During hard times, we are tested. Difficult times are when our Guru's teachings become practical, like a lab. Here, the Court of Wajeeda was the lab where the Sahibzaday would practically apply the Guru's teachings.

Mother Gujri told the Sahibzaday about the Sikhs who gave their life but not their faith. She instilled the spirit of fearlessness within her grandchildren. Mothers, have we kept this spirit alive? Have we taught our children to be so strong that nothing can make them waver? Have we taught them to connect with God and stand for truth? Have we given them the gift of steadfastness in their faith? Have we taught our children not to fear anything, even death? The quickest way to destroy a society is by weaking its women. Mother Gujri Ji is the role model of what every Sikh mother should be. As mothers, can we look Mother Gujri in the eyes and say we followed her path? Can we say we even tried? Have we taught our children to love truth or have we ourselves gotten lost in materialism alongside our children? What are we raising? Mother Gujri is raising her children to be devotees or God, to be brave, to sacrifice, and serve society. Have we followed her path? Are we walking with our mother on the journey of shahadat. Have we passed down her blessings. All mothers love their children, but to be a Sikh mother is much more. A Sikh woman's heart loves all of humanity. Her maternal love is limitless. Where do we as woman stand on this path? What are our priorities as mothers, daughters, sisters, wives, and woman. Mother Gujri Ji is not most special for being the Guru's mother or wife, Mother Gujri is special for her Sikhi. She is Guru Gobind Singh Ji's Sikh first and mother second. She is Guru Teg Bahadur Jis Sikh first and wife second. A mother of the world may have held her husband back from sacrificing his life, she may have told her son or grandsons to comply with the regime. Even if the Sahibzaday had insisted on giving their lives, the government would have more than happy just to have Mother Gujri Ji convert. It was likely that the government would let the Sahibzaday go if Mother Gujri ji converted. The conversion of the mother of Guru Gobind Singh Ji alone would be enough to malign the Sikh movement. If Mother Gujri Ji fell weak, then we would not have Sikhi today. We must never forget Mother Gujri Ji's strength and her maternal love, and she fulfilled her duties as not a just mother, but a Sikh mother. We must never forget that as daughters of Mother Gujri Ji we have inherited Mother Gujri Jis great strength, it is up to us to embrace it and to continue her journey.

First Day in Court (11 Poh)

On the 11th of Poh, the guards came and separated the sahibzaday from Mother Gujri Ji. For a moment, just imagine a mother being forcibly separated from her 7- and 9-year-old children. If someone even looks at a mother's child the wrong way, the mother's heart beats fast. Mother Gujri Ji told Baba Zorawar Singh Ji and Baba Fateh Singh Ji to stay strong and that she will see them when they come back. The guards took the sahibzaday to the court. They believed that the sahibzaday were ordinary children and would be easily influenced if they were separated from their grandmother. They thought they could bribe and scare the sahibzaday into embracing Islam and becoming subservient to them. They did not know the inner strength and fearlessness of Guru Gobind Singh Ji's true Khalsa. Sikh writer, Bhai Vir Singh Ji, often stated that forced conversion through fear or bribery is a disservice to any religion. When you bring people into your religion through threats or bribery, then you are populating your religion with those who are greedy or those who are cowards. This is counterproductive and even harmful to a religious community. Forced conversions therefore end up weaking a faith or ideology, rather than strengthening it. It is the sacrifices of those souls who are free from fear and greed, which strengthen the roots of a movement.

The brave young princes of Guru Gobind Singh Ji walked into the Court of Wajeeda fearlessly, with smiling faces that shined bright with the glow of godliness. They had a purity in their eyes and walked like young princes. They carried themselves with carefree confidence, royal valor, and childhood innocence at the same time. With great courage, the young princes stepped into the court and greeted all with the Sikh greeting, "Waheguru Ji Ka Khalsa, Waheguru Ji ki Fateh," meaning, "The Khalsa belong to God and victory is always God's." All the government officials in the court, all the governors, judges, and priests were shocked at this boldness, and that too from such young souls. Most children of this age would be crying for their mothers. Yet, these young warriors showed no trace of nervousness. Instead, they dared to greet the Court loudly with the Sikh greeting. This was a slap in the face to Wazir Khan and all the officials.

All around the court were thousands of soldiers holding weapons and spears. There were scary looking officers, yet these young princes walked in carefree. That is the way of God's devotees. Those who trust God never have to worry. They are always in Chardi Kala. *Nanak bhagta sada vigaas-* Oh Nanak, the saints are always merry.[68] When a toddler is learning to walk, they are afraid of falling down, even if their height to the ground is less than a foot. Yet, that same toddler laughs with joy when their father plays with them and throws them in the air over his head. That same toddler is not afraid, even if they are six feet in the air. They have trust that their father will catch them. This is the trust that a devotee should have in the Lord. Even in times of trouble, they should know that they are in God's safe hands. They should never lose their confidence, even in a room full of enemies. As Sikhs, we may be in places where we are judged. We should remember our brothers during those moments, and we should hold our heads high with the same confidence. We too are the sons and daughters of Guru Gobind Singh Ji. When we face hardship or judgement, we should remember this scene and the confidence of our brothers. When we do that, the sahibzaday will walk with us. As we walk on their journey, they will all accompany us on ours.

---

[68] Guru Granth Sahib Ji, 2

On this first day of court, the officials acted very loving towards the sahibzaday. Wajeeda and his advisor, Suchanand, acted like they loved Sahibzaday. They spoke in soft voices and smiled at the sahibzaday. They told the young princes, "We want you to live. We will give you anything you ask for." In reality, the officials truly did indeed want the sahibzaday to live. They did not want to execute the sahibzaday. They wanted the Sahibzaday to live, but under the government's terms. It would be a slap in the face of the Sikhs if the sons of Guru Gobind Singh Ji left their faith for riches. On this day, the sahibzaday did not just stand up for themselves, they stood up for the whole kaum, for all of Sikhi. Had they wavered, it would be a loss for the whole kaum. Their victory was our victory. They carried the flag of Sikhi on their shoulders and took care of it so that future generations could live with this honor. They aced this test and the whole panth was rewarded with their certificate.

The officials kept attempting to implore the Sahibzaday to embrace their faith. They told them that they would give them riches for the rest of their lives. They even promised that they would give the sahibzaday their daughters' hands in marriage and reward them with government titles. Baba Zorawar Singh Ji and Baba Fateh Singh Ji said they already had everything; they did not need any titles or riches. They said their faith was worth more than any treasure that the government could give them. Each attempt to convert the sahibzaday was an attack, an attack of words. There was a war of ideologies going on in the courtroom, as the young princess stood tall and fought for the ideology of Guru Nanak Dev Ji. They stood up for freedom, equality, compassion, dignity, truth, and human rights. The government tried their schemes, and cunning tricks. However, the sahibzaday were able to defeat each attack and knock down the government's attempts at bribery. They may have been physically young, they may not have had the military strength of their enemies, but still they had the power of truth. This truth hurt those false leaders more than any weapon. The government officials realized that bribery would not work. They sent the sahibzaday back to Thanda Burj for the night. Baba Zorawar Singh Ji and Baba Fateh Singh Ji went smiling, with glowing faces, back to Mother Gujri Ji. They hugged her and told her that they were successful in Court today and passed the first test. They told her they stood tall and held tight to the teachings of Guru Nanak Dev Ji. They did not fear the cruel tyrants. The government's bribes and attempts to lure the princes with greed failed. The Sahibzaday stood tall in their faith and did not waver. With beaming faces, they showed their victory over greed, and came proud to Mother Gujri Ji.

Second Day in Court (12 Poh)

After bribery did not work, the government decided to change its strategy. They would try anything to convince the children of Guru Gobind Singh Ji to leave their faith. Today, the government officials decided it was no longer time to play nice. Today would be a day of deceit and threats. It would be a day of fear and force. Once again, the guards came and took Baba Zorawar Singh Ji and Baba Fateh Singh Ji away from Mother Gujri Ji. Mother Gujri Ji hugged the sahibzaday tightly and gave them her blessing. Mother Gujri Ji told the Sahibzaday that she will see them in the afternoon.

After the first day, the government officials were shocked that these young princes were not enticed by their promises. They had never seen such bravery before, not only was it unexpected but it was shocking. Still, the government had hope that even if bribery failed, threats would work. Even kings and brave warriors are afraid of death. These are just children, they thought. However, this is the childhood of Sikhi. Wisdom and bravery know no age in Sikhi. The government thought that the sahibzaday will be afraid and beg for their lives. Once again, the corruption, deceit, and threats of the officers failed to shake the resolve of Guru Gobind Singh Ji's princes.

The first act of deceit started even before the young princes entered the court. The officials had a small door cut into the larger door of the courtroom. This door was so small that the sahibzaday would have to bend down to come inside of it. The idea behind building this door in this way was that when the sahibzaday would bend down, their heads would bow before the Court. The children of Guru Gobind Singh Ji would bow before the cruel government. The same children of the Guru, who refused to bow the day before and greeted the court with a Sikh Fateh, would now bow down before the Court. The officials underestimated the wisdom of Baba Zorawar Singh Ji and Baba Fateh Singh Ji. They were indeed the children of the same Guru who made faces and refused to salute the cruel governor of Patna Sahib. They were the grandchildren of the same Guru who said that you should always keep tyrannical rulers at your feet and never let them get over your head. As the court officials waited for the young princes to enter and bow their heads, Baba Zorawar Singh Ji and Baba Fateh Singh Ji went through the door feet first, showing these cruel tyrants their place. Let us learn from our brothers how to keep our heads held high. Even today, there are those who want the heads of Sikhs to bow. Like our brothers, let us have the wisdom to recognize those entities and to only bow down before our Guru.

When Wazir Khan and Suchanand saw the feet of Baba Zorawar Singh Ji and Baba Fateh Singh Ji pointed at them, they could not believe their eyes. The whole room was shocked at the wisdom of the sahibzaday at such a young age. Wazir Khan and Suchanand took turns trying to scare the sahibzaday with lies and threads. Wazir Khan told the

109

sahibzaday that they had caught their father and that they had killed Guru Gobind Singh Ji. They told the Sahibzaday that they are now orphans, they are alone in the world. and that they had no one else to take care of them so they should convert, and they will be taken care of by the regime. They even said that Baba Ajit Singh Ji and Baba Jujhar Singh Ji had already converted and embraced Islam. Baba Zorawar and Baba Fateh Singh Ji did not believe their lies for even an instant. They were connected inside with the truth. Otherwise, imagine telling a young child these frightening lies. There is no age limit or minimum age for connecting with God. These young souls were connected to the truth in their core. Their faith was not based on blind rituals, it was based on the experience of God within. Gurbani says *"Those who have God within their hearts do not die. They are never deceived."*[69] In the past, those in power have tried to use deception to win over followers. This practice continues today. As Sikhs, we can use the example of the Sahibzaday to remind us to also be aware of those who use act like they have our best interests in mind, those who use the public's religious sentiments for their benefit, and those who spread lies to deceive followers into compliance.

The officials decided that today they would use deadly force if needed. They wanted the princes to beg for their lives. Wajeeda and Suchanand said out right that if the young sahibzaday do not convert they will be put to death. Not only will they be killed but it will be a terrifying and painful death. One beyond imagination. The Sahibzaday were told that the

---

[69] Guru Granth Sahib Ji, 8. Although people may take advantage of good people, Gurbani tells us that in the end the final victory will belong to those who stand with truth. Those who have God may lose in the eyes of the world but in reality they are always victorious.

torture they already faced will look small as compared to the way they will be executed.

Wajeeda and Suchanand asked the sahibzaday if they are not afraid of death. Baba Fateh Singh Ji asked Wazir Khan "Are you not afraid of God." They called Baba Zorawar Singh Ji and Baba Fateh Singh Ji *"kafirs"* or infidels. Baba Fateh Singh Ji explained that a true Muslim is one who is kind and honest. According to Guru Granth Sahib Ji *"Musliman Maum Dil Howay"* or *"A true Muslim is one whose heart is soft like wax."*[70] Guru Granth Sahib Ji teaches *"Tau Nanak Sarab Jea Mehramat Howe, Ta Musliman Kahaway"* or *"Oh Nanak, only when a person is merciful to all living things do they have the right to be called a Muslim."*[71] It is against Islam to kill children for revenge against their parents. However, these ruthless leaders were only using religion for their gain. The priests and officials may have had rosaries and been chanting "Allah, Allah, Allah" but they were far from Allah and true Islam. Like Gangu, they had religious knowledge. Outside they looked like religious leaders. Wajeeda had a Quaran, he held a rosary, but he was far from true Islam. Likewise, Suchanand looked like a Hindu priest on the outside but had no religion. Their actions not only made them sacrilegious, but also made them criminals in the eyes of their respective faiths. That is why it is important for Sikhs not to be deceived by those who look religious. Religion is not about clothes. When Guru Nanak Dev Ji went to Kartarpur Sahib, Guru Nanak Dev Ji took off his religious garb and wore the clothes of the world.[72] This tells us that religiousness is not in clothes or worlds. Gurbani says, "bhekh anek agan nahi bujhai" which means that wearing religious clothing does not extinguish

---

[70] Guru Granth Sahib Ji, 1083
[71] Guru Granth Sahib Ji, 141
[72] Vaaran Bhai Gurdas Ji, Vaar 1, Pauri 38

one's inner fire.[73] True religiousness is in thoughts, intentions, and actions. Otherwise, anyone can easily dress up and call themselves a man of God.

That day, there was one true Muslim in the room. Wazir Khan had called in Sher Mohammad Khan who was the Nawab (Viceroy) of Malerkotla. Two of Nawab Sher Mohammad Khan's brothers were killed fighting in battles against the Sikh. Wazir Khan told Sher Mohamad Khan that he should take revenge for his brothers' deaths. Wazir Khan said that Sher Mohamad Khan should decide how Sahibzaday will be punished. Sher Mohammad Khan was outraged at the suggestion that he would avenge his brothers' deaths by killing the innocent 7- and 9-year-old sons of Guru Gobind Singh. Sher Mohammad Khan said that it is not permitted in Islam to kill innocent children for revenge against their father. Sher Mohammad Khan said that cowards kill like this and if he wants to avenge the death of his brothers, he can do it fighting in a war. He then then left the room screaming "Oh Allah, save me from being involved in this sin." Till today, Sikhs remember his honesty with courage and love. We never forget his taking a stand for truth. There is a memorial gate at Fatehgarh Sahib named after Sher Mohammad Khan. It is on the main roadway and all who pass by remember his bravery. Even though Sher Mohammad Khan had attacked Sikhs before, and he had used harsh words, and even said that he wishes to twist the neck of Guru Gobind Singh Ji, the Sikhs do not forget his noble action. That noble action outweighs everything else, for the Sikhs. It is always important to value the virtues in our fellow brothers and sisters. The Khalsa always is forgiving and large hearted.

---

[73] Guru Granth Sahib Ji, 265

Once again, the room turned into a war of ideas. Suchanand told Wazir Khan not to keep the sahibzaday alive. He called them the children of snakes. He convinced Wazir Khan that letting the young princes go due to their age was foolishness. Suchanand said that even keeping them alive and imprisoned would not be wise. Wazir Khan then asked the sahibzaday what they will do if he were to set them free. Baba Zorawar Singh Ji and Baba Fateh Singh Ji bravely answered, *"We will grow up and challenge cruelty till the day we day."* This angered Wazir Khan and shocked every person in the room. Such bravery in the face of death by such young souls. No one would dare stand up to Wazir Khan like this! What are these children made of? They are not children. They are great saints in children's bodies.

For some hours, the threats, and efforts to convert the sahibzaday to Islam continued. The officials tried relentlessly. Two young souls shook the very core of thousands of so-called learned scholars and government officials. After hours of trying, Wazir Khan decided to try his last resort. He read out his verdict and sentenced Baba Zorawar and Baba Fateh Singh Ji to death. They young innocent princes were to be executed by being suffocated in a bring wall. The public was outraged. Such cruelty upon such innocent young souls. Yet the brave princes remained untouched. The smiles did not leave their faces. There was not a trace of fear. The sentence was read, and the brave princes once again went back to the Cold Tower victorious. The government thought that once Baba Zorawar Singh Ji and Baba Fateh Singh Ji told their grandmother that they were sentenced to death, that too in such a cruel manner, Mother Gujri Ji would be afraid and convince the sahibzaday to convert to Islam. Instead, Mother Gujri Ji hugged her blessed and beloved grandchildren, and applauded their bravery.

113

And they will Remove every Trace of Cruelty from this Earth.

The next day Mother Gujri Ji prepared her princes for their blessed destiny. She hugged them tightly one last time and combed their beautiful kesh with her blessed hand. The touch of a mother, the touch of a blessed saintly soul, is very powerful. It was with one touch on the head by scholar Bhai Vir Singh Ji, that Bhai Puran Singh Ji, who had gone on the path of atheism, was so moved that he became a great Gursikh scholar like Bhai Vir Singh Ji. Today, mothers have lost that love and care. They are quick to cut their children's kesh because it is hard to take care of. By cutting their children's kesh, they are disconnecting their children from their roots. Remember, Mother Gujri Ji, and how she lovingly combed her beloved grandson's kesh and gave them one last tight hug. Dear Mothers and fathers, and elders, life gets busy but always find time to lovingly care for your family. One embrace is powerful and can release a storm of feel-good hormones. When children see their elders pray as they comb the kids kesh, or make meals, when children are connected to their Gursikh elders, they will associate that love with Sikhi. Sikhi itself is love. No matter how stressful life gets, always take time to show care to those around you.

Baba Zorawar Singh Ji and Baba Fateh Singh Ji left the cold tower like handsome grooms, princes on the way to their wedding. The guards surrounded them on all sides. Mother Gujri watched with pride. Today, instead of saying I will meet you when you come back, Mother Gujri said go forth and I will come following you. Baba Zorawar Singh Ji and Baba Fateh Singh Ji walked, arm in arm, holding hands. Allah Yaar Khan Jogi Ji describes this scene using the word *"Naunihal"* which means full of joy. Like children laughing and playing, the princes walked towards their execution without a care in the world. Their faces radiant, their

114

youthful bodies full of glow, Baba Zorawar Singh Ji and Baba Fateh Singh Ji walked towards their fate saying, *"Sat Sri Akal, Sat Sri Akal, Sat Sri Akal (Truth never dies, Truth never dies, Truth never dies)."*

The government executioners, Shashal Beg and Bashal Beg, from the village of Samana, started building the brick wall around the sahibzaday. These executioners were the sons of Jalal -ud- Din, the executioner who beheaded Guru Teg Bahadur Ji[74] (the father of Guru Gobind Singh Ji/ ninth Sikh Guru). The executioners were also the grandchildren of Noor ud Din, the executioner who executed Guru Arjun Dev Ji (great-great grandfather of the Sahibzaday, fifth Sikh Guru).[75] Shashal Beg and Bashal Beg told the sahibzaday "Do not think that we will have any mercy on you because of your age. We do not have mercy. Our grandfather executed your great-great grandfather, and our father executed your grandfather. We come from a family of executioners. Our hearts will not show you any mercy. There is still time to convert and escape your punishment." The Sahibzaday replied *saying "If you are from a family of executioners, remember we are also from a family of great shaheeds, who gave their life but not their principles."* The princes said *"Hamri bans reet im aiye, sees daiya par dharam nahi jaiye,"* meaning *"In our family we have this tradition, we sacrifice our heads, but we do not give up the fight for righteousness." Just like you won't feel any mercy, we won't feel any fear.*

The executioners started building the wall higher and higher. When the brick wall reached the knees of the young princes, the executioners started cutting the bricks so that the wall could be built around the kneecaps. This would make

---

[74] See page 30 for account of Guru Teg Bahadur Ji's execution.
[75] See page 25 for account of Guru Arjun Dev Ji's execution.

the wall a bit crooked. The Sahibzaday told the executioners, *"The wall you are building to execute us, the wall you build around us to suffocate us, this is no ordinary wall. You are building the foundation of Sikhi. Make sure you build it straight, even it that means you have to chop off our kneecaps to build it."* This is symbolic of the fact that they suffered, they took all the pain upon themselves, to build the foundation of Sikhi.

The wall had to be built and rebuilt multiple times. The bodies of the princes were slashed with knives in multiple places, and their blood spilled out. Baba Zorawar Singh Ji and Baba Fateh Singh Ji were knocked unconscious several times as an attempt to frighten them by giving them a taste of what death would feel like. Once unconscious, the executioners would massage the palms of their hands to revive them. They would then ask once again if after the close brush with death the Sahibzaday were now ready to convert.

Allah Yaar Khan Jogi Ji writes about the moment when the wall suffocated the young princes to the extent that it started becoming difficult for them breathe and their blood circulation was slowing down, Baba Zorawar Singh Ji and Baba Fateh Singh Ji spoke to each other. They said this is a new kind of cruel torture. Baba Zorawar Singh Ji and Baba Fateh Singh Ji had heard about how their ancestors were boiled alive, set on fire, and beheaded, but this was the first example of being bricked alive. Then they exclaimed *"For us, we do not see this as cruelty; we see this as God's grace. We have been blessed. The more torture that happens on our bodies, the more Guru Nanak Dev Ji's ideology will flourish and bring hope to this dark world."*[76]

---

[76] "Shaheedan-e-Wafa," by Hakeem Allah Yaar Khan Jogi Ji, stanza 108.

Imagine the feeling your body feels when it is underwater. Recently during the Coronavirus Pandemic, many patients have described the terror of the body not being able to breathe. The body goes into deep panic for the next breath. It is one of the most terrifying feelings in the world. Each time Baba Zorawar Singh Ji and Baba Fateh Singh Ji stopped breathing, the wall was taken down and the young princes were brought back into consciousness. They were told, *"You still have time, embrace Islam and we will give you life."* Baba Fateh Singh Ji asked the officials *"You say you will give us life. Tell me something? The life you claim you will give us, wont that life also end in death? Is death not guaranteed?"* Baba Fateh Singh Ji then continued and said, *"Even if we were to live for 100 years, death is guaranteed. To live as slaves with our heads bowed down is beneath our dignity."*[77] Allah Yaar Khan Jogi Ji shares the dreams, the hopes of Baba Zorawar Singh Ji and Baba Fateh Singh Ji. Allah Yaar Khan Jogi Ji narrates the final words of these innocent souls who spilled their blood but refused to bow before cruelty. These words should pierce the heart of every Sikh like an arrow.

"Hum Jaan Daike Auro Ji Jaana Bacha Chalay

Sikhi Ki Neev, Hum Hai Siro Par Uthah Chalay

Guraiye Ka Hai Kisa Jaha Main Bana Chalay

Singho Ki Saltnat Ka Hai Pouda: Laga Chalay

Gadee Se Taajo Thakat Bas Ab Kaum Paaygee

Duniya Day Zaalamo Kaa Nishaa(n) Tak Mitaaygee

---

[77] Ibid.

117

"By giving our lives, we save the lives of others. With the bricks that bury our heads, we lay the foundation of Sikhi, and spread the message of the Guru throughout the world. With our sacrifice, we lay the soil, and plant the garden of the Kingdom of the Khalsa. Now, the Khalsa will capture the crown, rise to the throne, and vanish all traces of cruelty from this Earth.[78]

As Baba Zorawar Singh Ji and Baba Fateh Singh Ji said these words, the wall collapsed one more time. The tyrants then slit the necks of these blessed saintly princes. According to history, Baba Zorawar Singh Ji's blessed body took about two and a half minutes to attain shahadat. Baba Fateh Singh Ji's foot was shaking in pain for over twelve minutes until his small body attained shahadat. In the Thanda Burj, Mother Gujri Ji said a final prayer, and breathed her last at the same time that her beloved grandchildren attained the blessing of Shahadat.

The Cries of Princess Zaina Begum

Wazir Khan's wife, Princess Zaina, pleaded every day with her husband not to commit this cruel and depraved atrocity. Every night she fought with him, crying, and begging him not to hurt those pure innocent souls, who the princess referred to as beautiful flowers. Wazir Khan had also promised that he would not execute the young princes. As soon as Princess Zaina found out about Wazir Khans ruthless murder of Baba Zorawar Singh Ji and Baba Fateh Singh Ji, she felt a deep unbearable pain. Princess Zaina decided she could no longer live with a murderer and did not want to live as the wife of such a cruel, sinful, and demonic tyrant. Princess Zaina was in such agony and helplessness,

---

[78] "Shaheedan-e-Wafa," by Hakeem Allah Yaar Khan Jogi Ji, stanza 109.

she felt that she could not live another second as the wife of such an evil man, so she took a *khanjhar* (knife-like weapon) and stabbed herself to death.

The most expensive land in the world.

After the martyrdom of Mother Gujri Ji and the younger sahibzaday, the cruel tyrants did not allow for a proper cremation. A wealthy Sikh merchant of Sirhind, Diwan Todar Mal Ji, spent all his wealth to give Mother Gujri Ji and the Sahibzaday a proper cremation. Diwan Todar Mal Ji owned many boats, and his house, called Jahaazi Hawali, located in Sirhind, is even shaped like a boat. Diwan Todar Mal Ji was an international trader and had a lot of money. His family was blessed by Guru Teg Bahadur Ji, and Guru Ji told them that they would one day be given great sewa to perform. Diwan Todar Mal Ji made many efforts to obtain the blessed bodies of Mother Gujri and the sahibzaday. Diwan Todar Mal Ji had to cover the whole cremation ground vertically with gold coins as a payment to Wazir Khan, in order to obtain the blessed bodies of Mother Gujri Ji and the sahibzaday. Gurudwara Joti Saroop Sahib stands where the blessed bodies were cremated. Some time ago, elders had found the urn containing the blessed ashes of Mother Gujri Ji and the sahibzaday, and it was reburied at the same spot. Diwan Todar Mal Ji and his family had to leave their wealth and home due to the wrath of Wazir Khan over his cremating the bodies. This land is known as the most expensive land in the world, but it is not expensive merely due to the money. It is expensive due to the history and the love of Diwan Todar Mal Jee.

Sirhind becomes a pile of bricks.

Guru Gobind Singh Ji's letter to Aurangzeb, *Zafarnama*, hit Aurangzeb with the reality of his actions.

After King Aurangzeb died, Guru Gobind Singh Ji helped Aurangzeb's son, Bahadur Shah, fight for the throne. Bahadur Shah had come to the Guru asking for help. Sikhi always believes in justice and not revenge. Had Guru Gobind Singh Ji wanted revenge, he could have tortured and executed Bahadur Shah, the way that Aurangzeb had done to the beloved sons of Guru Gobind Singh Ji. Instead, Guru Ji helped Bahadur Shah become King. When Guru Gobind Singh Ji was asked why he helped another Muslim become King, after he had spent his whole life fighting Aurangzeb's cruel regime, Guru Gobind Singh Ji replied, *"It doesn't matter who the ruler of a nation is, or what religion he is from, as long as he rules with compassion and fairness."*

After the shahadat of the sahibzaday, a Muslim devotee, named Noora Mahi, told Guru Gobind Singh Ji the details of what happened. At this time, Guru Gobind Singh Ji pulled a weed out of the ground and said, "Just as I pulled this weed, my Sikhs will rid this earth of the cruel regime." Indeed, it did not take long for the Moghul Regime to come to an end. In 1710, not even six full years later, Sikhs, led by Baba Banda Singh Bahadur declared victory over Sirhind. The whole city was destroyed and conquered by Baba Banda Singh Bahadur Ji and his army.

Thus, the Moghul Rule of over seven hundred years ended in a matter of five years. Baba Banda Singh Bahadur Ji was also captured and became shaheed. Baba Banda Singh Bahadur Ji's four-year-old son, Ajai Singh was also executed. Baba Banda Singh Ji had his skinned pulled off with hot pliers. His son was also killed in front of him. At first, the executioner (Farukh Siyar) tried to force Baba Banda Singh Bahadur to kill his own son. Baba Banda Singh Bahadur refused and stated that a Sikh does not kill innocent children. Baba Banda Singh Bahadur also stated that he would never even kill the executioner's innocent child, let alone his own. After killing Shaheed Ajai Singh Ji, the executioners put the heart of Ajai Singh Ji in Baba Banda Singh Bahadur Ji's mouth to torture him.

That is the bravery of a Khalsa leader. No where else does a leader have the courage and strength to have his son killed in front of him and to taste his own sons' heart. The sacrifices of our shaheeds gave life and strength to the kaum. Sikh history is filled with examples like this. The women who were imprisoned and shaheed in the prisons of Governor Mir Mannu[79] were forced to see their children cut into pieces. They were forced to wear the severed limbs of their children around their necks. It was the cruelty of the regime that led to their end. Even though the Sikhs were outnumbered, all it takes is faith, spirit, and the Gurus blessing. The Sikh heroes were Sikhs first and that is how they became heroes. They never forgot their principles even during battle. Sikhs never destroyed enemy places of worship. The Mosque next to the house of Wazir Khan still stands today. Baba Banda Singh Bahadur and the Khalsa army never attacked any house of worship because their fight was never against any religion. The Khalsa's fight was against tyranny and tyranny has no religion.

When Baba Banda Singh Bahadur started his mission, he had an army of only five Sikhs, and only five arrows, a Nishaan sahib, and a nagara. That is all it took to start. In each village, Baba Banda Singh Bahadur Ji made the kindest and simplest man the leader. This built confidence and made for compassionate rulers. Baba Banda Singh Ji is a great example of a Sikh leader, and we can still look to him for inspiration. As a General, his heroism is unmatched. Baba Banda Singh Bahadur Ji marched towards Sirhind gathering Sikhs. He would tell the Sikhs "Remember the

---

[79] Governor of Punjab, 1748-1753

wall of Sirhind." This would fill the Sikhs with spirit and passion. By remembering the wall of Sirhind, they found the courage and power to overthrow the regime that had ruled for over 750 years! They walked behind the Sahibzaday on the journey of shahadat, and kept the Nishan Sahib flying, and the Nagara beating. Today, let us also remember the wall of Sirhind. This will give us the strength, courage, and power to fulfill our purpose and walk behind our brothers, our Khalsa family, as we join the journey of Shahadat.

EPILOGUE: THEIR JOURNEY IS NOW OUR JOURNEY. HAVE WE KEPT THE FAITH?

When Guru Gobind Singh Ji found out from the love filled Sikh, Bhai Noora Mahi Ji, about the sacrifice of Mother Gujri and the younger sahibzaday, Guru Ji looked at the Sikhs and said the famous words *"So what if four sons have been shaheed, thousands of my children are still alive. I will see my children in my beloved Sikhs."* In Zafarnama, Guru Gobind Singh Ji said to Aurangzeb, *"So what if you have killed my four sons, my khalsa remains as a coiled snake to challenge cruelty. You have put out a few sparks, but the flame (my khalsa) is still blazing."* My dear sons and daughters of the Khalsa, you are that flame! You are the vessel which carries the strength of those that came before you. You are the descendants of the throne of Baba Zorawar Singh Ji and Baba Fateh Singh Ji. Once you surrender to the guru, you take birth in the home of the guru, and you become a Sikh by your actions, then the spirit of the sahibzaday will shine within you as a guiding light. This spirit will give you the strength to fight against millions. This spirit will turn you into a force of good. It will turn you from a victim to a defender. This is the challenge of the blood spilled by your ancestors, this is your heritage, this is your family.

Today we must carry on the mission of Baba Zorawar Singh Ji and Baba Fateh Singh Ji. Baba Zorawar Singh Ji and Baba Fateh Singh Ji had this faith in their kaum, in us. They told the cruel tyrants with pride that future Sikhs will prosper and fight, so that every trace of cruelty is gone from the world. Today, each Sikh has a mission to stand tall like Baba Zorawar Singh Ji and Baba Fateh Singh Ji. We must honor their sacrifice and fulfill the trust they had in us; a trust so deep that they gave their lives. They thought us worthy of this deep trust. In the eyes of the Guru, we were worth sacrificing the sahibzaday. How special is that? How precious are we? As Sikhs, we are blessed to be the descendants of such brave warriors.

125

However, today, Sikhs have become detached from their deep roots. We are so much more than what we have become. Instead of healing the world with the revolutionary message of Guru Nanak Dev Ji, we ourselves have lost that message. We must awaken ourselves to the deep love that is found in the house of Guru Nanak Dev Ji. The love for humanity that inspired our shaheeds to sacrifice everything. We must fight our egos and embrace our confidence. We must stand with pride as the children of the great warrior-saint, Guru Gobind Singh Ji.

Today, this world needs the universal message of Sikhi more than ever. It is time to take the Gurudwara out of the four walls of a building and into society. We must open our arms to those who society has shunned. This world is suffering in pain and hatred. There is cruelty and apathy in all directions. Greed has taken the place of love. People step on others to get ahead. No one cares for the meek. Humans have turned into monsters. They cause others misery and are themselves miserable. Religious people have become hypocrites. They act like they own God and spread hatred in God's name. It is only the revolutionary love of Sikhi that can heal this world and bring forth Guru Gobind Singh Jis dream, the dream of *haleemee raj*, the Kingdom of Compassion.

In order to bring forth the vision of Guru Gobind Singh Ji, each Sikh needs to fight with all of their strength. Guru Gobind Singh Ji taught us that fights are not only fought with weapons (hathiar) but they are also fought with the pen, with ideas, and knowledge (veechar). Many times, the pen can accomplish what the sword cannot. At Chamkaur Sahib, the elder sahibzaday and gursikh shaheeds fought a battle with hathiar. They fought with swords, guns, cannons, and other weapons. In the court of Wajeeda, the younger sahibzaday fought a battle with veechar. They fought with words, ideas, knowledge, and confidence. It was a battle of two ideologies. A battle of freedom and slavery, love and hatred, acceptance and fanaticism, closed-mindedness and becoming universal. Today, most Sikhs are physically safer than they were in 1704. We are no longer living in jungles. Many Sikhs now live in democratic Western nations, where they are free to practice their faith. However, our ideology is not as safe.

Today's battle is very much a battle of veechar. We must fight to protect the philosophy of Guru Nanak Dev Ji. Today, Sikhs have migrated all over the world. We must shine our light and share our ideology wherever God has placed us. Each Sikh is an ambassador of the Guru's universal message. Sikhs may live in different places and work in different fields, yet we have the same mission, to make this world compassionate and to lovingly serve God's creation. Wherever God has placed us, we must use our talents to fight our *Dharam Yudh.*

Each Sikh should strive to educate themselves, develop themselves, and excel in their fields. Whatever talents they are blessed with, they should work hard, reach as far as they can, and use their talents for the betterment of humanity. Whatever career they have, they should do it with love and compassion. They should live out the teachings of Sikhi in their work. No matter what a Sikh is doing, or how they are serving, they are always a member of the Khalsa army, the army of compassion, the family of Guru Gobind Singh Ji. This is their identity. Whatever job a Sikh may have, they are a saint. Whatever job a Sikh may have they are a soldier. A Sikh doctor, who heals without distinction, who serves with love, that doctor is a soldier. That doctor is fighting Dharam Yudh. That doctor is making this world better. That doctor is spreading kindness and nurturing others. That doctor is working honestly and not chasing after greed. That doctor is walking the journey of Guru Gobind Singh Ji. That doctor is fighting to turn this world into haleemee raj.

Likewise, the lawyer who fights for justice, the lawyer who challenges tyranny, the lawyer who ensures their clients never go unheard, that lawyer is a soldier. That lawyer is making this world less cruel. That lawyer is protecting the meek. That lawyer who is fearless in challenging power, that lawyer who is honest and not greedy, that lawyer who takes the side of righteousness, that lawyer is fighting Dharam Yudh. That lawyer is furthering the vision of Baba Zorawar Singh Ji and Baba Fateh Singh Ji and working to eradicate every trace of cruelty from this world.

That teacher, who teaches their students to love and serve is fighting for haleemee raj. The teacher who puts the spirit of compassion into young minds is working to eradicate cruelty from the Earth. That writer or artist who uses their talent to awaken the morality of the public conscience is a soldier fighting for haleemee raj. That businessman who is honest and sincere, who shares what he has with the less fortunate, is a soldier fighting for haleemee raj. That mother or father, who raises and teaches their children to be brave and compassionate, to walk the journey of Baba Zorawar Singh Ji and Baba Fateh Singh Ji, is a soldier fighting for haleemee raj. That child who stands up for those who are bullied, who embraces children that are picked on and less fortunate, that child is fighting for haleemee raj. That student who studies as hard they can so that they excel and make this world better, is a soldier fighting for haleemee raj.

That politician who shuns corruption and serves with kindness is a soldier fighting for haleemee raj. Scientists, engineers, preachers, waiters, farmers, janitors, poets, writers, veterinarians, artists, environmentalists, no matter the field a person is in, they all have the potential to be soldiers fighting for Dharam Yudh. They all have the potential to struggle for haleemee raj, for the dream of Guru Gobind Singh. It doesn't matter if the battlefield is a warzone in an armed conflict, a courtroom, a hospital, or a classroom, if every Sikh performs the duty they are blessed with in a manner that is consistent with the teachings of our Guru, this world will automatically become haleemee raj. All we have to do is stay true to who we are as Sikhs, and lovingly act in that manner.

In order to stay true to our identity, we must first always remember who we are. Our Guru gave up his family to make us kings and queens. However, today we act like we have become beggars. It is sad that even children of Sikh families have turned to drugs and alcohol. When someone is intoxicated, they are no longer in control of themselves. One who is not in control of themselves is not a king, they are a slave. Some drink and take drugs to escape their pain. This is also not the Sikh way. A Sikh faces their problems and struggles. A Sikh fights against their mind constantly. Today, many who live in great comfort are falling into depression. We have forgotten *Chardi Kala*. Even when Sikhs had the constant fear of torture and death over their heads, they were peaceful and thankful. Today, even the smallest stress causes great anxiety. Even those born in Sikh homes have given up struggling. The lessons of the ancestors have been forgotten. The children of leaders have started to become followers, trying to be like everyone else.

Guru Gobind Singh Ji said, *"Jab lag Khalsa rehai Niara, Tab lag Tej Deo Main Sara,"* meaning *"As long as my Khalsa stays distinct from the ways of the world, I will give them all my strength and brilliance."* Sadly, many have lost their identity and followed the ways of the world. Even those who wear a turban or bana, they look distinct on the outside, but inwardly they are no different than everyone else. A Sikh is never ordinary. A Sikh must live extraordinarily. A Sikh must love extraordinarily.

Gurbani talks about the current state of our kaum, in this line *Nirpat ek singhaasan soeaa supane bheya bhikhaare. Achhat raaj bichharat dukh paaeyaa so gat bhee hamaaree,*[80] *meaning "The King falls asleep on the throne and dreams that he is a beggar. He is separated from his kingdom and endures pain. This is our condition."* We are all royal. We are all strong. We are all the brothers and sisters of Baba Zorawar Singh Ji and Baba Fateh Singh Ji. We are all of a beautiful lineage. We are all loved by Guru Gobind Singh Ji. Even if we have fallen from the path of the Guru, Guru Ji is waiting for us with open arms. The state of us begging from the world is just a dream. Our sadness is just a dream. Our weakness is just a dream. Our reality is that we are the beautiful princes and princesses of the Khalsa army. We are the beloved children of the King of the Universe. Guru Gobind Singh Ji's power is always with us. When Guru Gobind Singh Ji left his physical body in 1708, Guru Ji told Sikhs that from now onwards they were to consider Guru Granth Sahib Ji as the embodiment of the Guru's soul. The same soul, the same light, the one light, which passed down from Guru Nanak Dev Ji now lives in Gurbani. The light of Guru Gobind Singh Ji lives in Gurbani. All of Guru Ji's power lives within Gurbani and when we have Gurbani in our hearts, we have Guru Ji's power inside us. The Khalsa is the body of the Guru. Gurbani is the soul. When a true Khalsa is connected to Gurbani, nothing in the world can stop them.

After Guru Gobind Singh Ji left his body, it was the first time Sikhs were left without a human guru. Many Sikhs missed their beloved Guru and some even felt sad. The Sikhs

---

[80] Guru Granth Sahib Ji, 657

then remembered the words of Guru Gobind Singh Ji. They remembered that Guru Ji promised that he would be with them forever in the form of Gurbani. The Sikhs did ardas and asked Guru Gobind Singh Ji to speak with them. They told Guru Ji, "We miss you, where are you, Guru Ji ?" They then took *hukamnama,* they opened Guru Granth Sahib Ji to a random shabad, so they could hear Guru Gobind Singh Ji's reply through the shabad. Low and behold, the hukamnama which came was *"Sad Hazur, Hazur hai Najar, Kathay na Paiyo Duryiye,"*[81] Guru Gobind Singh Ji through Gurbani told the Sikhs *"I am always with you, I am always present, there will never ever be any distance between us."* Guru Gobind Singh Ji, in his eternal shabad roop, confirmed the faith of the Sikhs.

Guru Ji is always with us through Gurbani. If we want to connect with Guru Sahib, we have to internalize Gurbani. Without connecting to the Guru, a Sikhs life is worthless. In order to fulfill the mission given to us by our guru, in order to reach the state of bliss, in order to lose the fear of death, and in order to live to our full potential as kings and queens, we must connect with the shabad and let it transform us.

When people describe Gurbani, they describe it as peaceful. Gurbani does give peace. However, Gurbani is also dangerous to some. To those who wish to oppress and enslave, Gurbani is dangerous. Especially, for those who are religious or political leaders. Prior to Guru Nanak Dev Jis time, religion was used to divide. Guru Granth Sahib Ji unites everyone, from all castes and religions. Prior to Guru Nanak Dev Jis time, religion was used to make people afraid. Guru Granth Sahib Ji makes people fearless. Religion was used to control and enslave. Guru Granth Sahib Ji makes people free. Religion had been used to put some people

---

[81] Guru Granth Sahib Ji, 1000

above others, to make some people feel like sinners. Gurbani uplifts everyone, and helps those who sin find their inner goodness. Religion was used to give power to the leaders. Gurbani gives power to the downtrodden.

Gurbani is powerful. Gurbani is dangerous, just ask Jahangir. Gurbani is dangerous, just ask Aurangzeb. Imagine, a King being so afraid of Gurbani, that he calls a meeting to discuss the prayer "Asa di War."[82] We have such a powerful shabad guru, yet we do not understand how to connect with Gurbani. We do not know the power of Gurbani. We are disconnected from our energy source and have become helpless. Imagine how powerful and precious Gurbani is, that our Guru felt keeping Gurbani alive was more important than keeping himself and his sons alive. Our shaheeds felt Gurbani was worth being tortured and executed for. Our elders suffered so we can have these incredible teachings, yet so many don't even know what the pages of Guru Granth Sahib Ji contain. They don't know the treasure that is within these pages. They treat Guru Granth Sahib Ji as an idol. That is why it is incumbent for the youth to sit and talk with their Guru. It is important to read Gurbani and learn what your Guru is teaching you. That is the only way that inner strength can be found and shared with a world in desperate need of it. Each day this world gets darker and more violent. Each day people are angry, miserable, and depressed. Creation is burning in despair. It is up to the Khalsa army to save it. Yes, we are all part of the Khalsa family. This is our first family. However, today we have made our families small. For a Sikh, the panth is the biggest family. Guru Ji lives in the panth. Guru Ji created the panth to care for all of creation and to bring love and peace to the

---

[82] Asa di War is a Sikh prayer which is read during mornings in sangat. Aurungzeb discussed Asa Di War with Ram Rai, the son of Guru Har Rai Ji, because he was concerned with the message.

world. If the panth is strong, then all of creation will be lovingly looked after. "Raj Karega Khalsa," is not just a blessing, it is a responsibility the Khalsa has to all of God's other children. How are we going to beautify the world if we ourselves are lost following it?

It is up to the youth to turn away from the ways of society, and the evils that have lured the generations before us and made them forget Sikhi. We must learn Gurmukhi and treat Guru Granth Sahib Ji like our Guru and not like an idol. Guru Granth Sahib Ji has the power to turn a human being into an angel. Guru Granth Sahib Ji does not just tell us to believe in God, but leads us to have a relationship, a connection with God. Through, Gurbani we know God, experience God, and even become God. We beautify ourselves and beautify the world around us. This is the true meaning of life. The meaning of life isn't riches or fame. Guru Gobind Singh Ji already had fame, wealth, a big family, and a comfortable house. Guru Nanak Dev Ji already had all these things the day he came into this world. If those things were the purpose of life, the Gurus could have stopped there. Sadly, many people keep their goals small. They aim for these material pleasures only. They never realize life's greater purpose.

Today many Sikhs unknowingly engage in emotional *beadbei* of Guru Granth Sahib. When someone physically disrespects Gurbani, all Sikh hearts hurt, as they should. However, each day those who call themselves Sikhs emotionally disrespect Guru Granth Sahib Ji. They emotionally disrespect the sacrifices made by Guru Gobind Singh Ji. When we claim to be Sikhs, but blatantly disobey and ignore the wishes of our Guru, this too is beadbei. For example, Guru Gobind Singh Ji's battles with the Hill Chiefs were fueled by Guru Ji's refusal to discriminate against those who were considered low caste. Sikhs laid down their lives fighting but refused to engage in casteism. Yet, this disease of casteism has made its way into our houses and sadly into our Gurudwaras. Guru Granth Sahib Ji speaks against dowry because it is disrespectful to women. However, this practice has also creeped into our homes and Gurudwaras. Judgement and ego have clouded our thinking. Slowly, the ways of the world are penetrating the Sikhi of Guru Nanak Dev Ji. It is up to us to use Gurbani as the blueprint of how we live our lives.

The strength of our ancestors was their connection to Gurbani. This connection gave them strong character and unbreakable spirt. We must reignite this connection. We must not just read Gurbani like a mantra, but we must understand it, and live it. The Sikhs in Anandpur Sahib did not just read "I will worship you whether you give me pain or pleasure"[83] but they lived it. Bhai Khanaiya Ji did not just read "Noone is an enemy or a stranger,"[84] but he lived it. Baba Moti Ram Mehra Ji did not just read "What does it matter if my body is cut apart? If my love for you goes, only then should your servant be worried," [85]but he lived it. What are we living?

Once Gurbani is in our heart, it transforms us. It gives us power to challenge cruelty and laugh in the face of death. Gurbani teaches us to live in high spirits and keep fighting for a better world. Today, so many live depressed and hopeless. Gurbani has the ability to bring life and passion inside those whose spirts the world has killed.

---

[83] "Je sukh dheh ta tujheh araadhee dhukh bhee tujhai dhiaaiee"- Guru Granth Sahib Ji, 757
[84] "naa ko bairee nahee bigaanaa"- Guru Granth Sahib Ji, 1299
[85] "kahaa bhio jau tan bhio chhin chhin.

In order to move forward, we must look back. We must look at Guru Nanak Dev Ji and his revolutionary love. We must look at the institutions which our Gurus built and developed. Sangat was once a place of love and acceptance. Today, judgement and hatred have crept into our gurudwaras. There is still time. The teachings of Sikhi have the ability to turn this world into a warm and blissful home for all of creation.

For a Sikh, walls are very symbolic. They symbolize the boundaries we must break on our spiritual journey, whether those boundaries are outside or us or in our own minds. When Guru Nanak Dev Ji started preaching equality, elitist priests tried to murder him by pushing a wall on top of him. Gurbani teaches that there is a spiritual wall of ego and falsehood which separates the human from God. Wazir Khan tried to silence the message of Guru Nanak Dev Ji by suffocating the younger sahibzaday in a wall. Sikhs must work to break the walls and divisions which separate humanity, whether they are walls of caste, religion, biology, lineage, these keep humans from loving all as God's children. We must also fight against the walls inside of us, the walls that block our potential, whether they are walls of doubt, fear, or anger. These walls limit us and make us mental prisoners. Like the younger sahibzaday, we must not let the walls we face stand in our way of our journey. Let us too open our hearts, embrace all of humanity, tear down the walls which imprison us, and continue the Journey of Shahadat.

135